It All Comes Down to "W.E.!"

It All Comes Down to "W.E.!"

A Solid Work Ethic is Key to Your Success

Linda Westcott-Bernstein

authorHOUSE®

AuthorHouse™ LLC
1663 Liberty Drive
Bloomington, IN 47403
www.authorhouse.com
Phone: 1-800-839-8640

Cover Design/Graphics: Susan Harroff, N2L Creative LLC

Published by AuthorHouse 12/27/2013

ISBN: 978-1-4918-4238-6 (sc)
ISBN: 978-1-4918-4237-9 (hc)
ISBN: 978-1-4918-4236-2 (e)

Library of Congress Control Number: 2013922534

CONTENTS

Dedication

This book is dedicated to my family, all of whom have stood beside me during times of challenge *and* growth. I want to especially thank my husband, Jeff, who has provided the inspiration, his writing and editing talents, and many years of patience and understanding, particularly of late, when I was not so sure that I would manage to finish this book and was worried if anyone would want to read it. I will always love and cherish you as the life partner that you are for me. You have made my life complete!

PREFACE

This book is a passion for me because of my years of work in the human resources field. I have always felt a great satisfaction seeing the "ah ha" light go on for people when they learn something new. Over the years, I have encountered many frustrated, misdirected and unmotivated people floundering under poor leadership, which is characterized by poor work and moral ethics. I have come to realize that my future lies with helping people reach their full potential.

It has also been my experience, over my many years in human resources (departments), that we get an unearned reputation as the "paper pushers" in most companies. Human resources is seldom treated as a partner in the success of the company. This is unfortunate, because the true success of any company lies with their people, those who do the day-to-day work. In reality, human capital is our most valuable asset.

It has been my passion over the years to help move the human resources profession in the right direction. I firmly believe that human resources should have a valued seat at the proverbial "table" and that they can have an enduring impact on the profitability of any company. When the people in any company are treated with respect and find satisfaction in their work, they will treat customers well. Remember, this satisfaction emanates primarily from the treatment of them by their supervisors. When you can ensure respectful treatment of your people, I believe that you will be on the road to success.

Work ethic is based upon the common sense values of focus, follow-through and team effort, and is supported by the belief in the importance of respect, fairness and ethical treatment. Won't you join me in my endeavor to change our future for the better? With a solid work ethic—the sky's the limit. We can do anything when we understand that work ethic is the key!

INTRODUCTION

A solid work ethic is the number one factor that has contributed to my life's success. From a very young age, I was taught the value of hard work and focus. As a child in the early sixties, I remember picking long rows of green beans in the hot summer sun. To my mind, these rows of beans seemed to go on forever and the work would never be done. However, my Grandmother and my Mom both spoke of the virtues of working hard and finishing a job completely. They also taught me that "many hands make light work"—when we all pitched in to get the job got done, the work went more quickly.

Now, picking green beans was just one chore among many that our family completed on our small farm in the upper Midwest. There were many other essential chores that also needed to be completed. One of the more physical tasks was baling hay. In the late summer, when the hay had been cut and dried by the sun, my Dad would hook up the tractor and baler with a flatbed wagon hitched to the back. Then my sisters (Lorrie, Louise or Lisa) and I would position ourselves on the wagon to stack the bales. We would hold on to the backboard of this wagon as the tractor pulled the entire rig around the field, bumping and bouncing over the rough furrows. We hung onto this wagon waiting for the first bale to come shooting through the baler and onto the flatbed. As Dad drove around the field, he would line up the baler intake with a row of recently cut and dried alfalfa. These bales would fly through the air, sometimes narrowly missing us, and land with a thud on the wagon. Then we would take turns picking up these 30+ pound bales of hay and stacking them on the flatbed. The hay needed to be stacked neatly, in multiple levels, so as to fit several dozen bales onto the wagon. As we rode around catching bales and stacking them, we'd be breathing in all kinds of chaff and dust in the process. This baling task would continue for hours, as we worked from the back of the wagon forward until it was full. It was hard, physical work for girls but we did it; most times with little or no complaining.

Now, this hay baling had an important purpose. Our animals: cows, horses, and pigs counted on this hay for feed year round. We knew, from many important discussions, that it was part of our responsibility to the family—to help keep up with the work on our farm. Over the many years it became quite evident that we each played an important role on our farm, and we each had to carry our own weight.

We came to understand the value of contribution and even felt good about doing our part for our family. Dad and Mom taught us that we must focus our efforts and build a solid work ethic in order to make our way in the world. From those lessons we came to clearly understand that hard work was worthwhile in our lives. Those lessons, the skills I learned and my belief in their value, shaped the person I have become today.

When you get right down to it, as I'd watch my Dad work in the fields, barn or garage, and my Mom cook, can vegetables, and clean house, it all seemed pretty natural and felt right to me. Observing their work behaviors over the years enabled me to gain a perspective of who and what I wanted to be. My desire to have a solid work ethic helped me to establish my foundation of sound decisions, actions and accountability. It was through those beliefs and ultimately the actions I took and decisions I made, that my character was molded into one that valued focus and achievement. This conditioning and many other essential lessons served as an introduction to a solid work ethic. I came to understand I could take pride in achieving the things that I worked hard for in life. Thus began my life of learning about and embracing the value of a good day's work. Out of those learning experiences grew my solid work ethic of today. I may have stumbled a couple of times, but overall it has served me well. I am thankful for my family and those many wonderful experiences which led me to today. I will always be grateful!

"Just Horsing Around"

When Dad was a young boy, he lived on a farm where there were horses and cows. In his day it was important that everyone, including their farm animals, pulled their own weight. Well, they owned a spirited but lazy horse that liked to break out of the pasture, trot down the road, and visit with the mare down on the next farm. This horse would escape by jumping the fence and eagerly trotted down the road to flirt with this mare. Dad was always tasked with fetching this horse back, and it did not make him happy to have to go after this animal time and again.

This horse had his role on the farm. His job was to pull the plow through the fields and cultivate the soil for planting each spring as well as to turn under the soil in the fall. Since he did not like to work, he would do whatever he could to avoid his chores and make it challenging for Dad to rein him in and follow along behind him on the plow. This clever horse had a mind of his own and would snort, spit and act extremely stubborn when it came to plowing the fields. It was funny though, as Dad had noticed, this lazy horse always seemed to have enough energy to jump over the fence and get down the road to the mare's pasture without difficulty.

Many years went by with Dad having to deal with this frustrating horse. One day, my Dad's father, was out working in the pasture mending fences when he noticed the horse lying flat out on his side on the pasture grass breathing slowly and somewhat labored. He walked over and took a look, and determined that the horse must be sickly and would have to be put down. Grandpa went back up to the house and told Dad that the stubborn horse was lying sick in the pasture and would have to be shot. Since neither wanted the task, Grandpa called Uncle Orrin to come over and put the horse out of its misery. The only concern was that Uncle Orrin was not a very good shot. But Uncle Orrin assured grandpa that he would take care of the sickly animal and set out for the pasture with his shotgun. It wasn't much more than 10 minutes later when Grandpa and Dad heard a gun-shot ring out from back in the pasture. As they both looked out toward the field, all of a sudden from over the hill they saw the supposed sickly horse racing as fast as it could toward and into the barn.

When Uncle Orrin got back up to the house he told them that he had lifted his gun, pulled the trigger and shot at the horse missing it completely. The horse had been so frightened that it immediately jumped to its feet and took off at a break-neck pace. Uncle Orrin said that he was amazed at how quickly the animal had recovered, gotten to its feet and raced off toward the barn to get out of sight. As it turned out, that horse was not sickly or tired, it was just lazy. From that day forward the horse had a changed attitude about work around the farm. It worked for another 12 years before finally succumbing to old age.

Lesson: One can do everything in their power to avoid hard work, but when reality comes knocking at your door; might the lesson be more difficult than the work?

FOREWORD

It is my intent, through this book, to communicate the importance and value of a solid work ethic in a light-hearted manner. I ask that you bear with me on this and enjoy the many unique references to the symbols of my childhood as well as my historically structured, business approach to disseminating information.

You will find that this book on W.E. (work ethic) is intended to communicate personal methods for gaining work ethic; however, it also outlines many business applications.

My focus was two-fold: 1) to help build individual work ethic, and 2) to show how work ethic can be applied in personal and business situations. The first section of this book, W.E. Foundations, is a reflection on personal experiences that contributed to my work ethic strength, as well as to examine and understand the circumstances which have contributed to the lack of work ethic in society today. The second section of the book focuses on Building W.E. (work ethic) and has a distinct structural content, however all of these concepts are presented in such a way to be applicable in personal situations. The third (and last) section of this book, Maintaining W.E., also has a structured style; however, you will find that these concepts apply in all parts of your life, especially your career or a business situation.

I hope you enjoy this book and learn to "Be Smart" when it comes to your future. You too can start counting your little piggies and take "W.E., W.E., W.E." . . . all the way to the bank.

"W.E." means "Be Smart!"
You "Build" work ethic.
You "Earn" respect.
You "Show" faith.
It "Means" trust.
You "Act" with understanding.
You "Reward" learning.
It "Takes" effort.

WHY "W.E."?

(Work Ethic)
Why is work ethic so important to you and (y)our future?

What for . . .
- People are unable to focus.
- People do not care.
- People do not want to put forth effort.
- People will take the "easy" route when given a chance.
- Work ethic has all but disappeared.

Why . . .
- We need to bring back the lost art of focus.
- We need to rebuild our national pride and instill shared goals.
- We need to return "Made in America" to its rightful place in the economic market.
- We need to transform our future workforces into capable, productive individuals.
- We need to get back to being the customer (not just a consumer).
- We need to build a culture that takes pride in work that is done well.

Because . . .
- Work Ethic becomes evident in improved performance.
- Work Ethic results in better customer care and service.
- Work Ethic offers learning, opportunity and growth.
- Work Ethic results in increased self esteem.
- Work Ethic leads to profitability!

Why W.E.? Because work ethic holds the key to our future success.

"W.E." IS YOUR KEY TO SUCCESS!

(Work Ethic)

Work ethic is success! It is about putting your skills to work to make personal strides, individual performance better, customer service better, and the company better. It's about improving your bottom line because everyone is on board with what the goal is, what is expected of them, and where you are heading. It's about being better than your competition! It's about profitability!

W.E. is a foundation—it's your roots! It is also your inspiration. W.E. feels exhilarating, motivating and exciting. W.E. compels you to get going every day and makes you ready to face the challenges of that day. W.E. represents your compassion, consideration and understanding. When you have faith and trust in yourself, you can achieve anything.

W.E. is a mindset. It is a way of life. It is a feeling deep down inside you that tells you to . . . "try again, try harder and don't give up!" More precisely, W.E. is that driving force that keeps after you to . . . "stay at it—you know you can do it!" A solid work ethic can bring you all the best things in life because you have earned them.

W.E. is also a choice, and it is up to you to choose a solid work ethic. W.E. is full of possibilities, and it only takes your imagination to make things happen. It may surprise you to discover that you never really know what you are capable of until you try.

So, get out there and "Be Smart." Make W.E. your key. A solid work ethic is your key to success. In the end, it all comes down to W.E.!

SECTION 1

"W.E." Foundations

CHAPTER 1

"W.E." Historically
How "W.E." got to where we are today

Historically speaking, work ethic has always been the key to our success. In times of strife; war for example, we have historically come together as a nation to achieve a common goal, support one another and change our future. It would seem to me that today we have forgotten history—maybe even lost our focus. But it doesn't have to be that way. True work ethic is characterized by individual and group effort. Work ethic will help us take back our future and that of our children.

I'd like to take a brief, nostalgic look back at those factors in our recent history that have contributed to the lack of work ethic today. As we look back at some of the behaviors that have affected our W.E. today, we will be reviewing the following topics.

- Setting the stage.
- Too much focus on "me."
- Poor role modeling equals poor efforts.
- W.E. can turn things around.
- Getting back to basics.

Setting the stage.

Today is such a different world than the one our parents knew. You could say that our parents generation had vision. Their generation embraced the concept of working hard to earn your way. We have learned their work values, which were founded on a solid platform of beliefs and standards, which everyone embraced and understood. Remember the philosophies back in our parents day; "You should rise early and go to bed when the work was

3

done." or "The early bird catches the worm!" For so many people in those days, their work ethic was a symbol of their worth to society. Many believed that work ethic defined who you were and that it was a measure of the quality of your character. And, interestingly enough, they were right!

Better still was the fact that back in our parents day, no one looked down on the man (woman) who toiled for long hours in the fields, the factory or the docks. In those days, their rough appearance was a badge of honor. That badge said . . . I work hard and earn my way. Hard-working people were highly regarded. Often unspoken was the wise proverb that "you only get what you desire if you are willing to work for it." There was no "I deserve this" way of thinking. Those were good philosophies.

In many ways, their support of hard work created a foundation for a solid work ethic that was revered and was in part responsible for bringing Americans closer together. Our parents' generation firmly believed that in America the sky was the limit. They believed they lived in a country where anyone could achieve anything if they were willing to work for it. This ethical work foundation was also apparent through the many unselfish acts of kindness, compassion and caring that their generation was known for, including rebuilding homes or barns during times of crisis, welcoming new neighbors with a basket of food for their home and going to church together as well as gathering afterwards for potluck meals. Those foundational beliefs set the stage for work ethic success.

Impact of WWII

A major historical event which served to bring our nation closer together was the war. During WWII people came together as never before. Emphasis was placed on the importance of us all pitching in to help our soldiers and the nation. While most men went to war, many women left their kitchens and went to work. For the first time, women worked on the assembly lines in factories. As our war efforts continued, men finally accepted the role of women in the workplace, and this shared effort helped establish a foundation for a new joint effort. This was a unique time for Americans, and it helped create a new focus and instill national pride.

After the war, our parents' focus turned toward raising a family, earning their way and laying foundations. Many of them focused their sights on a home, a steady job, and an automobile, and were not afraid to work for them. Those dreams would establish a goal for America's people. Once established, their work ethic would become unstoppable and lay the foundation from which any dreams could be realized. Over time, the American work ethic became known worldwide, a standard for people and cultures everywhere to strive for. "Made in America" meant quality. And with those first steps behind them, the American work ethic officially came to be.

Boomers—A Headstrong Generation

As I've said, our parents were a hard working generation, responsible and focused on providing a future for their kids because it was what they had learned. They found satisfaction in the value of earning their way and the benefits it offered in esteem and pride. They were bound and determined to teach us those traits and to give us that very same work ethic pride. And so, during the 50s and 60s, they set about to teach us all they could about work ethic.

However, the task of molding our character wasn't going to be a simple one. We were a headstrong generation and determined to find our own unique way and follow our own path. We decided that we wanted to experience sex, drugs, and rock and roll. Many of us became the hippies of the 60s and 70s. We spoke out against war and inheriting the ways of our parents. We didn't like the things our parents did and we turned a blind eye to their advice, values and beliefs. Along the way we had selfishly decided that our individual needs would come first and that we wouldn't work as hard as our parents did to receive our rewards. It became quite apparent, rather quickly, that their work ethic was not going to be our work ethic.

Today

Now, fast forward to today. There are about 78 million baby boomers born between the years of 1946 and 1964. I am, and you may be, one of those boomers. We are officially the "me" generation. We spent many years selfishly focusing only on our own needs. Instead of teaching our children good work ethic characteristics, we showered them with possessions and technology. We failed to instill in our kids the value of hard work with the same vigor our parents tried to instill in us. It is only now becoming apparent how deep the impact of this lapse in judgment may go. I suppose to some we thought we were doing the right things. We perpetrated so many selfish acts, with very few positive outcomes, that in the end we created challenges for our kids, the workplace, and society in general.

So, what will be the outcome? Whether you agree with my version of events or not, I ask you, what is the prognosis for our work ethic going forward? As I watch the news or experience what "service" has become today, I find myself asking these types of questions . . .

- Where has satisfaction gone in completing a good day's work?
- What has happened to the honor, pride, and ethics of the past?
- Why do we hold in esteem, those "icons" who have not earned our admiration?
- What does the future hold and where do we go from here?

These questions are not easy ones to answer and are the basis of and purpose for this book. It is my belief that we need to get back to basics, back to family values and back to work. I intend to show you how we can do just that. But first, I want to share with you some stories on my path to establishing my own work ethic.

A Glimpse at my "W.E." Experiences

My chores and responsibilities at home on our farm prepared me to focus, never quit, and always finish a job, or so I believed. In reality, some of the work experiences that were to come in my life helped me to grow, mature and learn much more than I would have expected. However, the reality of those lessons would only become clear much later in my life.

My very first job at the age of 14, was as a blueberry wrangler. I picked blueberries on a farm near my home town. Blueberries grow best in a wet, boggy soil and usually in a patch of land which is mucky and muddy. The work was backbreaking, bending over and reaching into thick bushes in the hot summer sun. In this work, you are always plagued by flies and mosquitoes and their constant biting and buzzing could drive you crazy. I would get paid a whopping $2 for a full pail of berries after spending at least two hours working to fill that pail. However, at the end of the week when we got paid, all my frustrations were quickly forgotten as I glanced at $50 cash. Visions of what I would spend my money on danced in my head. This was my first experience earning a wage, and I was proud to have my own money. I have to say I learned the lesson of perseverance in that job.

I was all of 16 at my next job. I worked in the clothing department of a local grocery store called Rumeries. I would spend hours working alone in a windowless upstairs clothing department opening boxes of shirts (or similar) and tagging them with price tags. Then I would hang them on the clothing racks or fold them neatly for the shelves. When there was no new stock, I would spend countless hours straightening, re-folding, and sorting the many stacks of socks, shirts, shorts, tops, pants and more. It was monotonous work but really not too difficult. It had its advantages, such as no hot sun, mosquitoes, or other insects. I also managed to learn a bit about customer service and running a cash register from a lady named Donna. There I learned the skill of "follow through and complete a job in its entirety."

When I turned 18, in 1974, I left home and moved to a big city for a job I had seen in the newspaper. I had excelled in High School (honor roll student) and had always held a great desire to see the world. I briefly attended a travel agent training school after graduation and then headed out on my own to experience life. But at age 18, in the mid 70's, you didn't get very far without a good work ethic. I soon realized that earning a living was not going to be so easy. In my first experience with a company called Greyhound, I learned my job, got paid weekly, and became a wage earner. I felt as though I had the world at my feet, and Chicago was my playground. However, reality quickly set in when I realized that living in a big city was expensive. My meager $191.00 take home pay every two weeks would barely cover my $200 studio apartment rent, $40 per month commuter train ticket, and also put some clothing on my back and food on my table. When money was tight, I frequently went without both of these items. I recall eating peas right from the tin can when I was about 19 years old because I was too embarrassed to tell my family that I didn't have enough money left from my paycheck to eat and survive. It soon became apparent that I would have to set my sights a little higher to get what I wanted out of life.

I then moved to a better paying job at another agency where I again learned to perform my job fairly well and seemed to excel. However, I still was young and didn't seem to grasp the concept of responsibility. I lost that job when I chose to call in sick on a work day morning from Los Angeles where I'd taken a spur of the moment weekend trip with my boyfriend. Needless to say, I was not grasping the concept of work ethic too well, but I did learn about commitment (the hard way).

My next job was at yet another travel agency but one where I worked with a very spiteful and nasty lady—or so it seemed to me. She would bark out orders, scowl and growl when things didn't go her way. She used all the travel perks that came into our office as sales rewards. I managed a couple of years under her regime and then moved on into another industry before learning everything I could about . . . "how I didn't want to behave as a boss."

My Turning Point.

Further along the way, in the late 70s and early 80s, I hooked up with a strange fellow that lead me down a path of abuse, indulgence and ultimately loneliness. This guy harbored some deep issues with women. He liked to spend his money, and could be generous at times, but he also had a sinister side. If his day had not gone well, he had a habit of verbally berating and criticizing those around him, even his girlfriend. I can remember being clearly informed one day that "I would NEVER be good enough to be his wife" because I was not of his ethnic background. As I look back today, I cannot, for the life of me, figure out what I found so enticing about this guy. I can clearly recall the day when I awoke and looked around at my surroundings and made a decision that was to forever change my life. I realized that I was worth more than all this abuse and degradation. So I gathered my belongings and walked out the door, never to look back. I knew I wanted to make something of my life and build a future of which I could be proud. That day was a turning point in my life, and I have never once regretted my decision or doubted that I made the right move. I certainly learned a lesson or two about self esteem from that awful experience, the most important lesson being to have faith in my own worth.

In this next section, I am going to explore those factors which I feel contributed to the shortfalls in work ethic with the current eX, whY, and Zzzz (my analogies) generations.

You may or may not agree with my opinion, but I believe it has to be said—

Too much over indulgence and focus on "me."

Our "me" generation has spent far too much time thinking only about ourselves, as was the case in my life. Those lost baby boomer years were spent wastefully over-indulging on selfish pleasures. We got carried away with our need for individuality. This distraction was a significant factor contributing to our lack of parenting of our children and eventually fueled the downfall of work ethic.

As time went by, our baby boomer generation found focus and turned our attention to work, but it came at a hefty price. As we married and settled into a job, we became more determined than ever to make up for lost time. Many of us toiled for long hours, worked weekends and spent numerous days away from home on business trips, in order to give our families the things we believed they wanted. Eventually, those misguided efforts backfired as the long hours kept us away from the very families we were trying to ingratiate. Those errors and quirks of fate kept us boomers distracted for many years. We missed what was important: our families; but we didn't realize just how important this lapse in judgment would be.

This lack of judgment was not surprising however, when you consider that many boomers tended to act like part-time parents, placed their kids in day care without a second thought, and succumbed to pressure from colleagues/careers to be more available. Some boomers have confessed that they would justify their "workaholic" behaviors by rationalizing to themselves . . . "I don't want my kids to go without as I did!" Those same boomers said they harbored resentment for being "shortchanged" during their childhoods when they were told that some toys weren't affordable and forthcoming.

To add insult to injury, the growth-spurt of the 80s and the technology boom of the 90s, made many boomers rich beyond their dreams and with much less effort than their parents. Some developed the mindset that they could "pass on" their acquired wealth—their affluence—to their children. This was not a good strategy. As a result of our expanding wealth, coupled with minimal parenting efforts, very little occurred to create a good family foundation and work ethic in our children.

These challenges with today's youthful workforce are not just coincidental. You see, our kids were given far too much, far too often. We are talking about kids that are accustomed to getting just about anything they want while knowing that they don't have to work for it. They've enjoyed abundance with no accountability. They expect things to come to them easily and do not fully grasp the concept of working for things or earning your way. When they enter the workforce, they end up acting out what they have learned. Because we have generations of ill-prepared, confused, and self-absorbed kids, we will be addressing these workforce concerns with them for the foreseeable future. We are now facing large numbers of kids that are poorly prepared to face the demands of a structured work environment. Of great concern is their lack of motivation as well as their inability to focus.

In many instances, these kids do not show manners and lack appreciation. Many act outwardly rude to customers, quit a job if they don't get what they expect, and have little patience for menial tasks or manual work, all because they lack proper ethical foundations. Most act in a spoiled, selfish and detached manner, and can be unmotivated most of the time. So the question remains, how are we going to deal with a generation of kids that lack focus and motivation?

Outcomes of Excessive focus on "Me."

The baby boomer generation was largely responsible for several of the following outcomes in our kids which have manifested themselves in character flaws, skewed values and poor work effort. This monologue of facts is being entered into, in an effort to raise awareness as to the mistakes of the past which have contributed to the situation we are facing today. We cannot lay the entire blame for this situation at the feet of boomers, but we made many mistakes that have contributed to our kid's current work ethic dilemma.

Chart of Excesses

Bad decisions made on behalf of our children.	
• They won't have to work as hard as I.	• They will get the things I didn't.
• I'll make their road a little easier.	• It was tough for me, why for them?
Excuses we've made.	
• It'll show my children that I love them.	• I am working so hard for them.
• They'll see how hard I've had to work.	
Our over-indulgence.	
• I've earned the right to pass on my success.	• Why shouldn't I have what I want?
• I sacrificed, so I can have anything I want.	
Outcomes of our actions.	
• Lack of basic family foundations.	• Lack of work ethic and effort.
• Children that are self-centered and selfish.	• Few family values, fewer morals.
Poor role modeling.	
• Poor parental guidance.	• No consequences for lack of effort.
• Poor moral base/foundation.	• No accountability.
• Poor "stick to it" attitude.	• Poor media figures as role models.
What we'll deal with going forward.	
• Children that don't make the connection between hard work and having possessions.	
• Children that don't value achievements, accomplishments, and contributions.	
• Children that have difficulty with motivation, self-esteem, and earning their way.	
Some challenging habits we'll battle.	
• Continuation of poor parenting roles.	• Sense of entitlement.
• Focus on material goods.	• Measure self worth by possessions.
• Skewed value systems.	

Here is a summary of outcomes our excessive focus on "me" (our selfish need for individuality) and our over-indulgence has had on our kids, ultimately resulting in such poor outcomes as little respect for parents, lack of appreciation, focus on fault and low motivation.

- Focus on possessions.
- Lack of desire or drive.
- Lack of motivation.
- Poor relationships, no commitment.
- Reliance on the media, television and the internet for identity.
- Sense of entitlement.
- Want, greed and selfishness.

We are dealing with a large segment of our population and a generation or two of individuals who exhibit a lack of resourcefulness and the motivation and desire to excel.

Additionally, about the same time that all this "me focus" was going on with boomers, society had stepped in and started to play its own role. The TV became babysitters for our kids. In the eyes and minds of our children, which were focused on the TV, those personalities developed into the role models which were missing. Their attention to the media became our children's security blanket, and had the effect of establishing false role models and transparent values, and ultimately glorified the rich. In the end, reliance on TV for guidance had the effect of destroying moral decency, subverted their sense of values and implanted unrealistic ambitions.

The final nail in the coffin came with the advent of reality shows. Our kids quickly identified with a litany of unethical, ill-conceived and outrageous reality shows which glorified bad behaviors, encouraged recklessness and destroyed private lives. Without our parental guidance, inserted at the proper time, our children were quickly engulfed in this pseudo-society where they were convinced they belonged. In the end, we failed to provide a quality family environment and establish a connection to those things that are truly meaningful in life.

Poor role modeling equates to poor service.

Many baby boomer parents didn't focus on or didn't know how to be a role model and instill sound social and working skills in their kids. Without those critical abilities, our kids were ill-equipped to maintain quality relationships, build self esteem, and develop any work ethic. When they are at work, our kids tend to be poor at focusing, lack an understanding of commitment and are poorly equipped to handle pressure.

In our efforts to make life a bit easier for our children, we overlooked the importance of nurturing those work habits which are inborn in all of us: drive, self esteem and confidence. Those unfocused and unmotivated individuals came into adulthood with skewed views of what the world expected of them and with very few values. In the end, many of today's kids have grown up without a sense of right or wrong and a lack of proper role modeling.

An unfortunate outcome of poor role modeling is the experience we now frequently endure that does not remotely resemble customer service. Instead of encountering individuals who understand and value the customer—to keep them coming back—we now endure those who assault us with rudeness, insolence and ignorance. Today's treatment of the customer, is a direct result of those impacts (sigh) that I keep repeating over and over: missing family values, poor role modeling, and lack of work ethic. And, somehow, it has become acceptable to put up with these unacceptable behaviors. Do you remember customer service? An obsolete term from the 20th century. Well, I do. We have unwillingly been transformed from "customer" to "consumer," and the experiences we endure reflect this unfortunate change.

Bottom line, we have no one to blame but ourselves for our misguided parenting efforts. Our kids are spoiled to such an extent that their moral compass no longer guides them. But we can do something to correct these mistakes in judgment. We can focus on work ethic and build new foundations with these future workforce members, our children. We must do it NOW!

What "W.E." can do to start to turn things around.

I believe that through the concepts presented in this book, much can be done to change the poor work ethics displayed by our eX, whY, and Zzzz generations. We can turn our poor role modeling efforts into an opportunity. Our goal must be to turn those unmotivated individuals, who don't seem to have a clue as to what hard work involves, into engaged and motivated workers. We will dangle the carrot of success in front of them and show them the way to a fruitful life with just a bit of effort on their part. In that way, they can have their cake and to eat it too! We will show our kids that work can be fun, and you can have your rewards too.

The key to rebuilding our future and regaining our pride is in building a better society founded on these W.E. standards and beliefs. It will require a shift in thinking, back to one of valuing honesty and hard work. But we must instill a sense of pride in work back into our children and thereby our nation. It is the key to our success and our future!

Let's Get Back to Basics

Our parents and grandparents took great satisfaction in building our country into the greatest economic engine on the planet. Their efforts shone as a beacon to all other peoples and countries. Through their hard work and determination of spirit, our forefathers and mothers turned their vision of "a land of milk and honey" into reality.

What W.E. need to do next is to get back to basics by bringing back the family unit, family values and our faith in things bigger than ourselves. W.E. need to express to our children, and each other, our love for and commitment to family as well as our desire for togetherness. As parents we need to provide positive role modeling and be involved in our children's lives and personal development. As parents we also need to make time for our children's interests, provide encouragement, and show genuine caring each and every day. These foundation—creating behaviors will help to restore our social fabric and return us to a give and take mentality.

As a society, we must live by morals, values and standards. These characteristics will only be properly instilled within others if we display them ourselves. A valuable step toward reaching your goals would be to outline your family's standards on paper and post them in your home. Your values and standards should be the positive things that you believe in such as honesty and faith. You should carefully evaluate what you believe in and then only pass on those values that are sound, support the greater good, and represent who you truly are.

Values are the principles that define who you are. Here is a sample list of Values:

- W.E. Love ourselves and one another.
- W.E. Respect one another.
- W.E. are always Honest.
- W.E. keep our Faith strong.
- W.E. Support one another.

A solid family upbringing should provide structure and boundaries, and be centered around your values and standards. If you live by your values, bring solid standards and expectations into your life and raising your children, you are creating a foundation for success, not just at home, but in all aspects of your life.

One of the many lessons I learned while I was growing up was the value of a good day's work and to have pride in my achievements. I found pride in accomplishing my work especially

16

when it would help me become stronger and wiser. When your accomplishments reflect your values, the result is positive psychological (mental) outcomes such as esteem and confidence.

Next we need Standards. Standards are those attributes that you live by and what you stand for. Here are some examples of Standards:

- W.E. do not steal.
- W.E. do not lie or cheat.
- W.E. work hard.
- W.E. respect others.
- W.E. learn from our mistakes.
- W.E. do not succumb to hate.
- W.E. try each and every day to be a better person.

Much of our values and standards are born from our faith: personal beliefs. Faith is a very personal thing. How we choose to live our lives comes from the strength of our faith. Ultimately, what lies within our faith-based beliefs will determine how good, respectful, and truly spiritual we are in times and situations where it really matters. You may not be God-fearing (that is ok)—however we all must be "good" people. That means good to ourselves, good to others, and good to our faith.

It seems to me that in recent times we have gotten away from those basic things that really have value in life and in the world today. We need to spend more time with family, teach our children our values, and show them the depth of our caring. We need to play a board game with the kids, talk at length about our beliefs, and tell a few tasteful jokes which elicit laughter from them. I am talking about genuine laughter, smiling, and hugging the ones you love, those things that are good for our mind, body and soul and really make us feel good about ourselves. We need to get back to basics and move our focus away from possessions, appearances and perceptions.

Now, here's a poignant story about values. This is about a family that got lost along the way.

Somehow They Got Lost.

I knew a family that had struggled early in life and had been dealt some difficult blows. The father had worked hard in his career but had succumbed to the effects of alcohol and had resultantly lost his job. This job loss and his spiraling downward due to his drinking broke up his family and left his children fatherless with a mother who was lonely and dependent upon her relationships for strength and guidance.

In a short time, she met a new man and she let her conscience, along with her rejected husband, fall out of the picture. This new man happened to be well off and was disciplined, materialistic and demanding. He expected her to look her best at all times (because, ultimately, her appearance was a reflection upon him), to keep her children in line, and to keep him in the manner to which he had become accustomed. This meant buying many "possessions" for him and their home— several expensive and rare items. Nothing was too good or too expensive. However, not too much time or money was spent on her kids. One important aspect of this new marital agreement was his blatant disregard and lack of affection for her children. To him they were just annoying fixtures and nothing more. They needed to be kept in line and out of the picture. Well, it didn't take long for his contempt of them to turn into aggressive behavior, resulting in one day yanking her daughter off the sofa by her hair. In his mind these kids were just a nuisance and a strict directive was placed upon this woman to keep them quiet and out of sight. They were also directed to never touch his possessions.

As fate would have it, one day she was placed in the position of having to make the ultimate choice between him or these children. Her kids were not towing the line and would have to go or he would leave her high and dry, taking along all of his possessions and money. Well, being as dependent as she was, she chose him over her own children. The children were tossed out of the house and her life like so much dirty laundry. They were pushed away from the one person they knew, trusted and loved— their mother.

As an aside, my children used to be friends with and spend time with these kids. We used to feed them often at our home and hear many sad stories about how they were rejected and neglected. We did our best to show them love and compassion, and I want to think that some of that love rubbed off on them— maybe just a little.

Where are these kids today you might ask? Well, they are young adults living tough lives in a very real world. Both have been in more than one bad relationship. Both seem confused, ill-prepared, and disconnected from society all because of their terrible home life. Now, someone please help me here. Would more standards, stronger faith and better parental guidance on the part of the mother have helped these children? Very likely. Could it have put these children on the right path toward success? Definitely.

What are some "basic" things that "W.E." can do?

Let's continue on this subject of "back to basics" by taking a look at some beneficial actions we, as parents, can take with our children to ensure a brighter future and a stronger foundation.

The main thing that W.E. can do is to return us to a life of basics and family-comes-first thinking. The foundation of a strong family is a great starting place and the key to the development of drive, self-esteem, and confidence in our future generations. With confidence, our kids can feel free to try new things, develop their creativity, and achieve more. You can help your children achieve their highest potential. They can do just about anything they can imagine. It all starts with you being there creating a solid foundation.

Next, we need to bring back pride in our family and pride in a job well done. We must all live by the standards and values we have developed. It is our role as parents to build that foundation that sets our children up for success. Start by making a commitment to your spouse to stay together. Work out your problems, argue less, show compassion, be flexible, consider another's perspective, and treat one another with respect. Show your children that what you stand for is commitment and teach them how to live up to their own standards. Be a role model by showing them that you are willing to work for what you want and that you are not afraid of a challenge. Instill work ethics in your kids that include focus, follow through, and pride in a job well done.

In summary, all along the way we need to be doing the following "basic" types of things which can steer our children in a better direction for the future.

- Spend time with your children, teach them patience, love and caring.
- Hold back those harsh, damaging words spoken in haste. Look for good in people.
- Be kind to your neighbor. Kindness to a stranger will come back to you tenfold.
- Be patient in traffic and in line at the store. Patience is a virtue.
- Call our parents more than just once per month. Talk with them and let them know that they matter and how they influenced our lives.
- Give time, once in a while, to a non-profit company or do something to better your community. Get involved.
- Attend your child's baseball game, dance recital or parent-teacher conference. Be present!

Lastly, we need to focus less on material possessions and pay more attention to our relationships. True happiness in life does not come from money, wealth, possessions or status. It comes from your heart. And your heart can only be happy when you know that you are doing the right thing, for all the right reasons, and have pride in the fact that you are honest and ethical. This is what we MUST teach our children. We have to get back to basics, listen to our heart and put our family above all else.

* * * * *

Readers please note I have inserted the following Capsule several places within this book as a reminder that ethical efforts and treatment of others is the key to your success!

> **"WE" Capsule:** Make sure your W.E. efforts always stay
> grounded in the foundational beliefs of respect,
> fairness and ethical treatment for all individuals.
> It is key to your success!

CHAPTER 2

"W.E." for You and Me.
The prospect for future generations

The future may be a challenging one when it comes to helping our children gain work ethic and motivational characteristics, but it is not an impossible task. Since we already are experiencing some of the pain of our past transgressions, we can and must focus on changing our future. As individuals, we'll have to make up our minds that it is time to change. Once we have done that, we'll have to set goals, find our motivators, and work together toward reaching these goals.

Our future workplace demographics will be made up of a wide array of eX, whY and Zzzz generations (my analogy) with a variety of motivations. The challenge will be to tap into those motivators with each and every individual.

- How we'll need to manage the future generations.
- What they'll have to do/learn.
- How we'll manage them going forward.
- How to tap into their motivation.

We have already talked about some of the challenges we will be facing with these "new" generations. Our ability to tap into what motivates these individuals will be the key to our and their success. We need to start now to instill pride, motivation and work ethic into our current and future generations. That will have to include some basic training on how to focus on a goal, follow through and/or how to stay the course to finish the job.

How do "W.E." manage future generations who have little or no "W.E.?"

W.E. will teach them! W.E. will show them how. W.E. will demonstrate how work ethic can lead to a happier, more fulfilling future. We have to demonstrate how there is reward, value in achieving things—in reaching for your dreams and attaining them.

For example, ask them . . . "Do you dread dealing with an individual that could obviously care less about you, the customer?" Remind these eX, whY and Zzzz generations of the possible outcomes when no one cares. Their future could look even more "me-centric" than ours did. It could turn out to be a very cold, callous place if W.E. don't instill some accountability and compassion. Ask again . . . "Does this scenario sound frightening to you?" It should! Without work ethic and focus, customer service ceases to exist.

Here are a few additional steps to help connect with the eX, whY and Zzzz generations:

- Give them some history of how we got here.
- Let them know they are not to blame.
- Demonstrate W.E. behaviors. Share some of the positive outcomes.
- Explain the potential returns and rewards.

You'll have to teach them the benefits of pride in working for something rather than getting things handed to them and show them the value of respectful treatment.

However, be prepared, you may have to do some "convincing" with these groups. They may need to be shown the benefits. Explain the reasoning for building work ethic and outline clearly the rewards of taking action. We must remember that we contributed to this situation. It may be tough to convince individuals who have little understanding and patience for work efforts. There will always be individuals who want to continue doing things the same as they always have. Yes, building W.E. will be toughest for those who don't embrace the value, rewards or outcomes of hard work.

What will the eX, whYs and Zzzzs have to do and learn?

When teaching W.E. you'll have to start from the beginning. Explain that it'll feel like starting over again. They'll have to learn the components of W.E. and to embrace the value of a good day's work. You'll have to go one step at a time. As you help them learn, you will need to be patient and compassionate.

- W.E. implementation should be broken down into segments.
  - o Introduction to W.E. (foundations)—why, how and when
  - o Keeping W.E. fresh and alive (building)—new, creative, adaptive
  - o Rewards of W.E. (maintaining)—original, valued, innovative
- Communication must be brief and concise.
  - o Tell them what will happen
  - o Tell them why it will occur
  - o Tell them when things will begin, continue, etc.
- Training should be timely and short—under one (1) hour (short/concise).
  - o Keep training to brief "snippets" of information each time
- Presentations must be unique each time
  - o Do not have a 'canned' approach. Be creative.
- Contents of communication must be original.
  - o Keep your audience's needs in mind. Use current language/expressions.
- Presenters must be confident and dynamic.
  - o Have only the most dynamic people present.
- Challenges and rewards must be imbedded in each step.
  - o Always give them something to strive for. Keep it fresh, unique.

Your eX, whY and Zzzz generations are more likely to succeed if they are taught in new and creative ways to keep their attention. The vision, mission and direction of your W.E. efforts must reflect current trends and be communicated in fresh and interesting ways. Your individual expectations and evaluation processes will need to be original and focused on individual contribution not always on the family, group or team. Lastly, the rewards must be valued and desirable.

These generations are not like those of the past. They are not fearful of leadership or repercussions if they don't comply. They are daring, challenge the status quo, and want to reach new heights. Gear your efforts toward the demographics of your audience and you are more likely to succeed.

How we'll manage them going forward.

Going forward, we will have to keep innovation and creativity high. You will have to blend teaching, coaching and learning W.E. components and standards with assignments that require original thinking and new challenges.

- Be innovative.
- Encourage creativity.
- Allow engagement.
- Offer challenges.

In many circumstances, these generations are not satisfied with the status quo or the same role every day. It will be important to keep your environment fresh, ever changing and focused on rewards.

This may sound like a lot of work, but it does not have to be. First, develop an ongoing internal marketing plan. Your marketing plan is how you sell someone on an idea or product. To be successful, you will need to sell your audience on why they need to have W.E. and the benefits of doing so (See Chapter 11). You will know that your marketing plan has worked when you notice positive trends. As a group, evaluate increased satisfaction and personal achievements, and then watch for a correlation between these two improvements. Some examples:

- At home, a positive trend in frequency of a clean room, toys picked up, or homework getting done without asking, means success.
- A teenager's successful efforts to be home on time, as requested by the parents, is nice progress.
- At work, a trend in improved completion of processing of returned goods may correlate to a trend in reduced customer complaints regarding processing of their returns.
- A trend downward in employee turnover may correlate with an upward trend in employee input on product lines and future company direction.

Next, in a business setting, you can develop a Diplomat program (see Page wherein select individuals become internal "cheerleaders" for your W.E. effort. Engage these Diplomat's by giving them some level of authority to affect change and reward efforts on the spot.

Also, maintain individual/group input and feedback processes and initiatives that are motivating, effective and responsive. Try current trends. Today blogging, texting, etc. are popular, however use those methods that connect with your audience.

How to tap into their motivation.

Motivate eX, whY and Zzzzers with involvement. Bring them into the loop by including their ideas and input. You will more readily identify with and motivate these individuals by setting new goals and levels of desired achievement on an ongoing basis. Remember, these generations have a lot of ideas to share and they want to be heard. Include a variety of initiatives such as the following:

- Discussion groups.
- Feedback tools.
- Open lines of communication.
- Opportunities to speak with leadership.

- New idea contests/competition.
- Suggestion programs.

But remember, you must implement some of their ideas from time to time as well as be ready to follow up with everyone. Otherwise you may lose their interest and possibly your credibility. It is, after all, W.E. for you and me.

Example.

At one company I worked with, the leadership wanted to keep their culture and initiatives fresh and motivating, so they were constantly improving and updating their reward systems. Their goal was to capture their people's ideas so they could increase sales, improve motivation and reward individual achievements. Their strategy worked. Their goal was to rotate their incentive programs. They got ideas from staff as follows.

1. Select your Reward. (day off with pay, CEO for a day, etc.)
2. Notice your Neighbor. (recognize your fellow worker)
3. What's your Thing? Cash, gift cards or credit. (rewards for your pocket)
4. LOL—Lunch on Leaders. (chance to be heard by leadership)
5. Build our Brand. (contest to encourage new branding ideas)

Originality is key with your efforts because you don't want anyone to become bored with the status quo. We all are constantly seeking new challenges and rewards, and an ever changing environment keeps us engaged.

> **"WE" Capsule:** Make sure your W.E. efforts always stay
> grounded in the foundational beliefs of respect,
> fairness and ethical treatment for all individuals.
> It is key to your success!

CHAPTER 3

One, Two, buckle my Shoe.
Work Ethic can be learned

Do you remember the nursery rhyme "One, two, buckle my shoe. Three, four, shut the door. Five, six, pick up sticks. Seven, eight, lay them straight?" It was a game we played as kids to help us learn or remember steps for a new task.

Yes, you can learn work ethic and help anyone else to do so also. Because the benefits of W.E. are so motivating, so rewarding, it will be easy to get others onboard. I believe that anything worth doing can be learned and by anyone. It is all in how you convey the information that determines the acceptance of the message. Here's what to do:

- You have to want to learn.
- For success, you must demonstrate W.E.
- Key W.E. concepts that can be learned.
- How to keep the learning alive.

Once experienced, the rewards of accomplishment and achievement are very motivating. You'll want more of it! It is like feeding a bad habit—but much better for you. There are no hangovers, no withdrawal symptoms. Just good feelings and good habits. And best of all—a great future!

You have to want to learn.

Before we commit to a belief or concept, people want to know what's in it for them. Just telling people to "do it, or else . . ." does not do the best job of inspiring others. You need to tap into what motivates them. Here are some of my personal learning motivators:

- Want more out of life.
- Desire for success.
- Time for change.
- Dreams of personal achievement.

Make sure your efforts for W.E. success focuses on those aspects of your life that you can and desire to improve. It is important that you keep your efforts and your goals realistic, attainable and motivating. One way to do that is to use my basic steps for setting goals (outlined in Chapter 4 under "Focus," one of five components of W.E.) to determine your plan. Be aware of the importance of laying out an attainable and well thought out plan. Don't expect to reach your goals too quickly. Here's a short story to emphasize this point.

Finding the Light.

I once emerged from a "fog" and found my way into the light. This transformation occurred physically, metaphorically and spiritually. My fog came about during a time in my life when I had no focus, no motivation and no goals. I also was plagued with low self esteem, need for belonging, and less than stellar decision making abilities. I was young and impressionable and began hanging around with a group of individuals who had destructive tendencies and chose to hide their insecurities in a fog of drugs, drinking and other less than reputable acts. One of the guys who was a leader of this pack admitted proudly one day that he had stolen money and jewelry from his mother to pay for the drugs and booze that he was "enjoying" that evening. He laughed, quite satisfactorily, actually about the whole thing, boasting to his friends about how he had pulled off this clever heist. That should have been a clear signal to me to get out of there, but unfortunately I didn't.

It took me a little longer to wise up. I continued to hang around and join in the partying. I experimented with drugs, joined in with the excessive drinking and flaunted the law, just so I could "fit in" with this group. It was truly a low point in my life. But I really hit the bottom one day when I found myself nursing yet another hangover, helping wasted addicts recover, and answering a call from the police that one of our group had been in an accident and was in jail for DUI. It was then that I started to ask myself why I was doing these things with these people.

Well, I did finally find my way out to the light. When I started to question what I was doing, where I was going, and what the future would hold for me, I realized that I did not like the answers. I realized that my life had no future and I was floundering on the edge of destruction. Deep down inside I knew I was worth so much more.

So I chose a day of escape when no one was around, picked up my meager possessions, and headed out the door to a new life. I decided I needed to straighten up my act at work, found a new apartment, and developed a plan for change. I never looked back and was never sorry that I made that important move toward the light.

For success, you must demonstrate "W.E."

Work ethic must become a part of all that you do and all that you are. When you get down to it, each of us must embrace and demonstrate W.E. in our own way. Here's some ideas to help you demonstrate and support your new work ethic:

- Post your "W.E. is the Key" quote everywhere.
- Share your W.E. standards with everyone.
- Communicate your W.E. values and expectations.
- Measure your success by honestly evaluating your progress.

Every document you prepare should reinforce and focus efforts on meeting your W.E. values and standards. Feel free to include others' ideas, changes and suggestions as appropriate. This act demonstrates that you value honesty and encourage input, and aids in the buy-in process with others.

Key "W.E." concepts that can be learned.

All of the following components and standards can be learned. They must become an essential aspect of who you are and all that you do. Here are some steps for learning and communicating your W.E. concepts.

- Start with family/group meetings. (town halls, assemblies, picnics, etc.)
- Build your W.E. culture from the ground up. (solicit ideas and creative thinking)
- Break your efforts down to the individual level and personalize it. (make it reflect your/their personality)
- Develop a W.E. newsletter or other communication. (keep everyone informed)
- Include your W.E. initiative in your Employee Orientation. (indoctrinate)
- Teach your W.E. expectations and goals to all leaders. (hold them accountable)
- Conduct W.E. surveys of staff. (ask questions, be sure to respond)
- Implement new W.E. job descriptions. (update your expectations)
- Expect individual engagement. (change is not optional)
- Measure performance against your W.E. standards. (be fair and consistent)
- Reward W.E. achievements, milestones and successes. (be visible, fun and valued)

W.E. is a great way to bring your goals to life. Then share those goals with your family and friends. These efforts won't have meaning unless they are fully embraced and supported by everyone you know and trust.

How to keep "W.E." learning alive.

One of the toughest challenges you may face, but one which is so important to your success, is to not let your W.E. efforts die a lingering death. The best way to ensure "life" to your W.E. initiative is to keep things real. Your W.E. effort has to include processes that are ongoing, genuine, comfortable, and practical. W.E. has to be supported sincerely by all members of your family and/or your business, and incorporated into all aspects of your life, and essentially it will become your new way of doing things. Here are some ideas for keeping W.E. alive in your life:

- Incorporate your W.E. values and standards into all that you do.
- Update your vision, mission and cultural messages to include your W.E. components.
- Be generous with your rewards for W.E. progress and accomplishments.
- Be aware and notice what is getting done, progress and personal satisfaction.
- Incorporate W.E. incentive efforts that are valued and worth striving for.

I have found over my many years incorporating new initiatives at large companies, that there is a desire to try the latest "flavor of the month" program (such as the latest fad diet, new technology or current trend) but with little attention as to the longevity and life of the program. When individuals or companies do not fully embrace or follow through on their intentions, your efforts are wasted and people become complacent. Everything they had hoped to achieve with the program falls by the wayside and dies.

To be successful at keeping your W.E. efforts alive, you must be committed to change, hold individuals accountable and measure progress. This way your efforts remain new, fresh and interesting. There must be encouragement for the free flow of ideas and your approaches must be constantly changing. There is a truism that few people embrace . . . "Who would choose the exact same path in life if we were given a second chance?" So why would it be surprising that we might desire change in our lives and environment too.

I also spoke about the importance of asking questions about what others find valuable, successful and most impactful regarding renewed work efforts. Here's what to do:

- Survey (ask) your people. (But not too often.)
- Act on their suggestions. (Don't ask if you don't act.)
- Make change your cornerstone. (Communicate your purpose)
- Set up a team/committee to oversee change. (Include all levels, rotate staff)
- Recommend and make changes. (Keep it new and fresh.)
- Reward and appreciate those ideas for change. (Engage staff, reward involvement.)

Your success at changing yourself, your staff and/or your future lies with your ability to engage the interest of those around you, follow through on what you start, and keep the momentum going through innovative and original approaches that keep everyone on the edge of their seats with anticipation for the next milestone. The message must be . . . "you are a key member of my/our work ethic-focused endeavor."

"WE" Capsule: Make sure your W.E. efforts always stay grounded in the foundational beliefs of respect, fairness and ethical treatment for all individuals. It is key to your success!

SECTION 2
Building "W.E."

CHAPTER 4

Building a House of Brick.
Creating a Work Ethic foundation

I remember clearly the childhood story of the three little pigs. One pig built his house of straw, hoping to keep the wolf out. The second pig built his house of sticks, thinking he was wiser still at keeping the wolf at bay. However, the third, truly smart pig built his house of brick, knowing after much thought and effort, that a solid foundation is the best defense against the wolf: representing the cold and cruel world.

We are now going to begin building our house of brick. We will do this by examining the foundational aspects of W.E. Here are the building blocks we will be reviewing:

- Where a good work ethic comes from.
- Why some have W.E. (take the W.E. assessment test.)
- Why some don't have W.E.
- The Five key components of Work Ethic.
- W.E. standards.

Where a good work ethic comes from.

The foundations of work ethic can be found in any person where the basic desire exists for success and achievement. Work ethic must be embraced in order to achieve those things you want and desire in life. It may be difficult for some eX, whY and Zzzzs to understand, but there is pride in completing a hard day's work and doing it well! When you have worked for or earned your way (rather than be given things), an innate sense of pride fills you with a good feeling about your sense of worth. That good feeling is the reward of a solid work ethic.

A good work ethic is not an elusive thing. To achieve success you must first understand the five components of W.E. They are present in all of us. The foundation or roots are found in faith, trust and desire. Desire is one of the key ingredients to achieving a good work ethic, and you must want success and all the good outcomes associated with it. W.E. is easier for some individuals to tap into. There are those who more readily recognize that work (both physical or mental) plays a key part in their future, and there are those who do not. But when you do find your desire, you must be willing to put forth the effort to learn and embrace the necessary skills. You will find that this foundation of knowledge and experience will always serve you well.

In the preceding pages I spoke about our country's history. Our country is a melting pot of races and cultures; immigrants came to America from all over the world searching for a better life. Many of them were fleeing the tyranny and oppression they had known in their own countries under various regimes or dictatorships. In those less than desirable environments, they had to work—and work hard. Unfortunately, it was almost always for the gain of someone else: a dictator, political regime, or socialist government. Seldom did the fruits of their labor result in personal satisfaction and positive gains. However, within these people was a spark and hope for a better life. They sought a place where they could decide how to raise their families, teach their children and enjoy the results of their hard work.

Because they were not afraid of hard work they began to prosper. In coming to America, they were able to leave behind those oppressive environments and apply their work ethic toward achieving their own goals and desires. This way of thinking set in motion a time of prosperity and great opportunity.

America was and still is "the land of opportunity." It is still true, you can do anything or be anything you desire here in America. All you need is the desire for success and a good, solid work ethic.

To quote Thomas Edison: *"Genius is 1% inspiration and 99% perspiration."*

Why Some have "W.E."

The first lesson W.E. students learn early is that life is not a free ride nor always fair. Life is what you make it. It reflects YOU and the choices YOU make in life!

W.E. people are those who have a good work ethic because they chose and embraced it and were raised with clear expectations, family values and good standards. They were told . . . "if you want something, you'll have to work for it." It's all in the family. My Grandmother Maude, my Mom's mother, is one of those people who had an abundance of W.E. She was born in 1913 and lived in Michigan, the seventh of nine children. Her parents were divorced early because her father was a drifter. She was born into a hard life and talked with us about the tough times during her childhood; the prohibition, the depression and the war. She wore hand-me-down clothing from her older sister and put cardboard in her shoes when the soles wore out. Her life was not easy and seldom fair, but none the less, she maintained a positive outlook.

Here is a quote from her life's story about her childhood . . .

"We couldn't afford any toys so I'd always borrow my neighbor's roller-skates. For fun we played baseball in the street with the other kids. In the summer we swam at the beach and went to the amusement park for just pennies. In the winter we got old car fenders from the junkyard and used them as sleds."

On the farm where Grandma lived there were many animals. There were dairy cows and horses in the pasture, calving stalls for the newborns, goats in their own pens out back, and chickens scattered all around the barnyard and house. These chickens not only laid eggs but served as a valuable food source for the family, as well as for the neighbors. One of Grandma Maude's messier tasks was to butcher the live chickens for cooking or for sale to the neighbors as needed. To my mind, Grandma seemed to have no fear. She knew what needed to be done and she got it done. This task was an unpleasant one. It required that you first catch the skittish birds, then hold them down while you took an axe to their neck, and then lastly hung them upside down from a nearby clothesline till all the blood ran out. It may seem a gruesome task, but it was a necessary one for survival back in those days. What I remember best about Grandma was her work ethic. She and grandpa ran a dairy farm in Michigan which had a huge red barn filled to the brim with hay to feed all of their cows. Grandma would get up at 5:00 a.m. every day and go to the barn to milk the cows. This was a physical task because there was very little mechanical equipment back then to assist them. To complete this tough job you had to wade through smelly, sticky manure to get the milking cows into the barn. You then had to herd them into individual stalls and lock a harness around their neck, all the while avoiding being stepped on or kicked by a mean or scared, half—ton animal. Next you had to reach under the animal and wipe their teats with an antiseptic to ensure cleanliness. Finally you had to bring the milking contraption down under the cow, hook up the milking tubes, and ensure all the lines were active and pumping the milk down the line to the collector. Grandma's work didn't stop at the barn though. There were always fences to mend and grasses to mow. She also had a great big garden and a root cellar filled with canned goods. Grandma cooked wonderful Sunday meals after church and played a masterful hand of Cribbage. Those were good times for me and I learned a lot by just watching her work their farm.

One valuable lesson that Grandma learned very early on, and instilled in each of us grandkids, was to work hard for those things you want in life. She'd reminisce of the challenges that she had faced in life and had overcome, and that we could achieve great things in our lives as long as we had the desire and the drive.

Another big influence on my life was my Grandma Anna, my Dad's mom. She was always hugging and kissing us, and talking about the importance of doing your chores before you went out to play. She put a lot of value on family, and she often used the phrase that I still remember and rely upon everyday . . . "Many hands make light work!" She knew if we all pitched in, the job would go much more quickly and easily for all of us. I remember her working in our large garden pulling weeds or picking vegetables in the heat of the midday sun. She never wavered in her task and always had a good word to say regardless of her exhaustion or our lack of effort.

Grandma Anna had a big orchard behind her house. There were apple, pear, cherry and peach trees. She would frequently make pies and coffee cakes after picking many of the wonderful fruits from this tree grove. Grandma loved cooking in her kitchen and the smell of something wonderful always filled the air around her home.

Grandma Anna was also very involved in her church. She would make an embroidered pillow or bake a pie, and take it to the church for one event or another. Grandma would always walk the three or so miles to the church for a pot luck and then back again after the event was over. Back in her day they did a lot of walking from place to place, since cars were a luxury. I remember her as always smiling and teaching us about the importance of doing our fair share of work around the house. Her wise words and gentle way helped guide and mold me into the compassionate and hard working person I am today.

Write down the names of people who have has influenced your life.

Name of Influencer	How They Influenced You
_____	_____
_____	_____
_____	_____
_____	_____

These important people in my life helped me to embrace the good feeling and rewards of achievement and accomplishment. I came to understand that those things I worked for and earned—I appreciated and valued more. My family; my parents and my grand-parents, helped me develop a sense of pride in a job well done. This pride blossomed inside me into a desire for success and created a willingness to put forth the effort to do all jobs well. I do not believe in "short-cuts." This work ethic is an integral part of who I am and is a road map for the future success in my own family.

If you take a moment to reflect on some of the stories of your life, I expect you may find you're a candidate for implementing W.E. in your life or career. Here are a few reasons for laying a foundation for W.E. success in your life too.

Top 10 Reasons for Saying YES to "W.E."!

1. Because it is easy to learn and do.
2. Because you have drive and desire.
3. Because you can see the success of those with W.E.
4. Because you can visualize a great future.
5. Because you are positive and proactive.
6. Because you are a doer, go-getter, and know what you want.
7. Because you like doing new things.
8. Because you know you are never too old to learn.
9. Because you take pride in a job well done.
10. Because you want to reach for your dreams!

> **"WE" Capsule:** Make sure your W.E. efforts always stay grounded in the foundational beliefs of respect, fairness and ethical treatment for all individuals.
> It is key to your success!

How do you know if you have the desire and capability to build your own solid work ethic? This is perhaps the most difficult step, your assessment step. You'll have to ask yourself some honest (and difficult) questions about what you want out of life. Just ahead is a work ethic assessment questionnaire that will help you to evaluate your options.

Some of the following questions may steer you in the right direction.

1. Do I care about how my life plays out?
2. Do I want to have control over my future?
3. Do I have the stamina to make change in my life?
4. Do I think (care) about the importance of what I do for others means?
5. Do I want to leave a mark on society/legacy for my family?

You also have to take a careful look at whether the following work ethic personality characteristics are present within you and assess those that you may need to build upon.

- Commitment
- Focus
- Follow through
- Honesty
- Persistence
- Structure
- Thoroughness

If your goal is to make a mark, remember that your mark on society (your legacy) does not have to involve any earth-shattering event or include winning a Nobel Prize. The most important marks on society are down-to-earth ones, including: making a commitment to your spouse to stay together, being there for your children, providing a solid foundation that nurtures success in those around you, being an honest and ethical person in life, and having friends and family around you who care about you because you care about them. There is so much more to leaving your legacy than notoriety. In our world, notoriety is seriously overrated! As I mentioned earlier, we have put people up on pedestals that have no business being there. And because of our lack of confidence, we allow ourselves to be influenced by those stronger-willed individuals. To my mind, the following expression certainly rings true . . . "the meek shall inherit the earth" because meek does not mean "weak" it means honest and true.

Nothing sticks to Teflon® Man.

The Teflon® Man was someone I worked with in the past. What I didn't know was life had not been very good to this man. He became known as the Teflon® Man because he made sure everything bad slid off of him and stuck to those around him. Since his main objective was to make sure that no negative outcomes could be attributed to him, he developed a sharp tongue and berated individuals in front of others. His motto was: "If what you attain is success, I will take the credit. If you fail, only you get the blame." He took credit for the work of others, without giving them credit for doing that work.

The ultimate irony is that everyone knew this about Teflon® Man. He continued to think he was untouchable, the center of the universe, while everyone around him wondered how competent could someone possibly be if they continually surrounded themselves with such supposed idiots?

The lesson with the most impact for me from this situation was to learn those characteristics and traits you never want to acquire. As you observe situations and watch people struggle under their own "Teflon Man®," know in your heart you would never want to become so jaded as to need to belittle others to feel good about yourself.

Lesson: The secret to success is in learning to treat others the way you'd like to be treated. Take a vow with me that you will come away from any similar situation with the most important lesson of all—do unto others as you would have them do unto you.

"Work Ethic" Assessment
What is your "W.E." score?

This assessment tool is intended to evaluate work ethic. Its purpose is to determine where you are on your path to attaining W.E. Answer the follow W.E. questions honestly and accurately. Remember, work ethic ideals may already be present in you.

Checkmark Yes or No for each:	YES	NO	Scoring Points
Are you pleasant to be around in the morning? Do you smile?	____	____	____
Do you make a list on paper/in your head of what you'll do today?	____	____	____
Do you make your bed (or other chores) consistently each day?	____	____	____
Do you conscientiously think about how your work affects others?	____	____	____
Do you begin your day by putting things in order at home/work?	____	____	____
Can you work as part of a team/group without having center stage?	____	____	____
Do you believe in the value of learning something new every day?	____	____	____
Can you finish a job all alone even when others should be helping?	____	____	____
Do you clean up at work/home before you finish for the day?	____	____	____
Do you have pride and a sense of accomplishment from your work?	____	____	____

Answer these Questions by Circling the Best Response:
(There may be multiple right answers, and a little humor, but only one answer exhibits W.E.)

Subtotal: ____

1. What are your first thoughts at the start of your day?

a. I gotta pee!   b. Whose life can I destroy today?   c. What will I accomplish today?

____

Questions - *continued*

2. *When you encounter a challenge in your work, day, or life, what do you think?*

a.   This sucks, I quit!   b. I'll wait till someone tells me what to do.   c. I bet I can figure this out!

    ____

3. *When everyone else takes off and leaves you doing the work, how do you respond?*

a. This sucks, I quit!   b. I can get this work done for now.
c. Everyone sure is lazy. I quit!

    ____

4. *If you are struggling with completing a project, what is your first thought?*

a. I'll get help.   b. Who can I throw under the bus?   c. No one is helping me!?

    ____

5. *When someone gives you a compliment for doing a good job, what do you think?*

a. Damn right!   b. Thank you! You are welcome!   c. Amazing! Someone noticed!

    ____

Subtotal = ____

Total = ____

Answers: See Scoring Guide (page 132) for assessing your W.E. score.

SCORING: Superior "WE" = 90-100 pts., Great "WE" = 70-89 pts.,
Average "WE" = 50-69 pts, Poor "WE" = 49 or less points

Why some don't have "W.E."

Those who don't have W.E. oftentimes have not applied a good work effort in their lives. Many people have lacked effective role models during their informative years: individuals who have displayed characteristics like focus, follow through, and perseverance. Yet for others, their motivation may not be focused and unfocused efforts are seldom productive. Then there are those of us who may be just plain lazy. Fortunately, I want to believe there are not too many of those kind of people. The key to effective work ethic is structuring your day/ life so that you can make progress toward your goals. This focused effort must involve the desire for success.

There are many whose lives are made up of I can'ts, constant disappointments and many excuses. They may be unsure how to proceed or freeze up out of fear of failure. They may have been told, far too often, they can't do something, won't amount to much or will never be good at anything. This is truly unfortunate. Whatever the situation may be, those who don't have W.E. oftentimes fail because they don't make the connection between learning these simple concepts and achieving more out of life.

Here are a couple amusing stories about "unethical" people (loosely based on real life). You may also have encountered similar people or maybe these stories just strike a very familiar chord with you. Any similarities in my stories to individuals or situations, real or imaginary, is purely coincidental.

If you are like me and can't understand why anyone wouldn't be on board with "W.E.," here is an example of someone who did not have work ethic(s).

On a bender with Cash Spender.

Cash was one of those self-centered and arrogant individuals who had managed to excel in his career primarily because of how well he could schmooze and convince individuals that he was an expert at whatever he did. You might refer to him as a "blow hard"—a big talker with not much to back up his exaggerations. In actuality, he was just over-compensating for his many shortcomings as a human being.

Cash did not like to work. He liked to take credit for other people's work. He wanted more than anything to be a big shot, but without having to earn the title. As I said, Cash would regularly take credit for the work of others and then provide this pseudo-work to his superiors and peers as if he'd gathered it. Oftentimes, his true colors would be revealed when he was asked specific questions about this work. I understand that he would stutter and stammer, not able to come up with plausible responses, and eventually he'd have to defer to his panel of "subordinates" for the concrete answers. Meanwhile he'd keep his subordinates at arms length from his superiors so their talents could not be identified.

Cash also liked to play favorites. He didn't concern himself with ethics and honor, he just wanted to be the big shot. He would create a small circle of insiders and then leave everyone else "shut out" having no inclination as to what was going on or if they would be allowed in.

Cash loved to play the big spender. When he traveled on business, nothing was too good for him, as long as he was spending the company's money. Cash was always generous with other people's money: indulging in expensive meals, gifts and entertainment at every opportunity.

One day Cash's actions caught up with him because he was habitual with his poor performance. His lack of results and unethical and flamboyant behaviors got the attention of his superiors when whispers of poor leadership, greed, and lack of integrity trickled down to them from his and other departments. It wasn't long before Cash was out the door for lack of effort, integrity and ethics, and for failing to live up to the standards of this company.

Lesson: You can try to live the high life as a big shot, but your lack of work ethics will leave you short on cash.

Ethel lacks Ethics.

You guessed it, this lady was not ethical. The business that Ethel managed consisted of travel arrangements for business and leisure travelers. She liked to run the show and be the big shot with all her well-to-do clients and corporate accounts. When clients came in she would put on a phoney smile, pour on the honey and fein that she would do anything to please them. However, after they left it was a different story. She would turn into a witch and start screaming out orders to her staff to do this and do that and do it now, in order to satisfy her clients. There was never a "please, thank you, or will you do this?" Just orders, demands, and temper tantrums. They did what she asked because they didn't want to get "berated" by Ethel.

Every now and then, the vendors for the travel destinations she and the staff would book for their clients would send complimentary tickets and other rewards to the office as a thank you for sending customers their way. Well, Ethel didn't care if she took care of the staff who took care of her. Not surprising, she had never learned to share. She would keep all the offers for herself— for her use during her vacation time. Sadly, the office staff had become accustomed to these selfish behaviors and not being able to share some of the fruits of their labor. In the long run, Ethel was found out for who she was. The parent company had received negative feedback on her from departing staff and along with high turnover it didn't take long for the company to catch on to these unpleasant trends. It seemed her days were numbered.

"WE" Capsule: Make sure your W.E. efforts always stay
grounded in the foundational beliefs of respect,
fairness and ethical treatment for all individuals.
It is key to your success!

Q. Do you have doubts about your ability to build work ethic? What is holding you back?

My Excuses Page
(Use this area to list and leave behind your doubts & fears.)

The things and thoughts that hold me back . . .
_____
_____
_____
_____
_____
_____
(May include your doubts, fears, concerns, etc.)

What I can do to overcome my concerns . . .

_____

_____

_____

_____

_____

_____

(Should include plans, ideas and motivations.)

Now, here are a few basic reasons some individuals might miss the mark with W.E.

Top 10 reasons for No "W.E."

1. Because we were never taught it.
2. Because we think we are not good learners.
3. Because we want a free ride.
4. Because we didn't/don't listen.
5. Because we didn't pay attention in class (life).
6. Because we have too many excuses.
7. Because we just don't care.
8. Because we can't visualize success.
9. Because NO is much easier.
10. Because that would take some effort!

These "No W.E." individuals can learn, but they'll have a challenging road to traverse to embrace W.E.

Remember the "Key to W.E." . . .

Work ethic is success! It is about putting your skills to work to make personal strides, individual performance better, customer service better, and the company better. It's about improving your bottom line because everyone is on board with what the goal is, what is expected of them, and where you are heading. It's about being better than the competition! It's profitability!

W.E. is a foundation—it's your roots! It is also your inspiration. W.E. feels exhilarating, motivating and exciting. W.E. compels you to get going each day and makes you ready to face the challenges of that day. W.E. represents your compassion, consideration and understanding. When you have faith and trust in yourself, you can achieve anything.

W.E. is a mindset. It is a way of life. It is a feeling deep down inside you that tells you to . . . "try again, try harder and don't give up!" More precisely, W.E. is that driving force that keeps after you to . . . "stay at it—you know you can do it!" A solid work ethic can bring you all the best things in life because you have earned them.

W.E. is also a choice and it is up to you to choose a solid work ethic. W.E. is full of possibilities and it only takes your imagination to make things happen. It may surprise you to discover that you never really know what you are capable of until you try.

So, get out there and "Be Smart." Make W.E. your key. A solid work ethic is your key to success. In the end, it all comes down to W.E.!

"W.E."
Five Key Components
"A Good Work Ethic"

The following five key components of a good work ethic will provide a road map for your success at developing, implementing and measuring W.E. ability and progress. These are the expectations to guide you, as you develop your work ethic lifestyle.

1. Focus on the job at hand.
   - watch, listen and learn
   - do what is expected
   - complete the job to the best of your ability
   - receive direction/correction effectively

2. Don't give up or quit.
    -   learn from your mistakes
    -   keep on trying
    -   don't be a quitter
    -   don't let challenges phase you
3. Share and bear the load.
    -   don't make excuses
    -   carry your own work load
    -   be present on the job
    -   pitch in willingly when others need you
4. Finish the job—completely.
    -   do all that is expected
    -   complete all aspects of your work
    -   don't do anything half-way
    -   clean up all messes
5. Take pride in a job well done
    -   have self-confidence and be proud
    -   perform your job with superior effort
    -   be genuinely proud of your successes
    -   share that "good feeling" with others

Always remember the goal—build a solid work ethic!

When you learn to embrace these five key components, you can improve your life! Give work ethic a chance and see how it changes your life. Remember to make sure your W.E. efforts always stay grounded in the foundational beliefs of respect, fairness and ethical treatment for all individuals. That is your key to success! My work ethic has positively changed my life and I am forever grateful!

"W.E." Standards
"A Good Work Ethic"

Measure your success with W.E. using these performance standards. Insert these standards into your performance evaluation process in order to gauge W.E. success. See "Tools" section for a sample form.

Scoring System (Pts.)

1. Focus.	20 Total points
a. Watches, listens well and learns.	5
b. Able to stay on task. Does what is expected.	5
c. Identifies what must be done and completes the job.	5
d. Follows instructions/directions. Pays attention to their work.	5
2. Doesn't quit.	20 Total points
a. Learns from mistakes. Keeps going even against adversity.	5
b. Stays the course. Keeps trying.	5
c. Doesn't give up. Not a quitter.	5
d. Doesn't let challenges distract them.	5
3. Shares and bears the work load.	20 Total points
a. A good team player. Doesn't make excuses.	5
b. Carries and completes their share of the work and then some.	5
c. Is mentally present at their job.	5
d. Pitches in without hesitation. Makes a contribution.	5
4. Finishes the job.	20 Total points
a. Does all as expected. Embraces the value of follow through.	5
b. Completes all aspects of their work.	5
c. No half-way work. Finishes up.	5
d. Doesn't leave work or trash behind for others. Cleans up.	5

5. Exhibits pride.   20 Total points
  a. Appears self-confident and   5
    self-assured.
  b. Performs job with superior effort. 5
  c. Genuinely proud of successes.   5
  d. Shares the "good feeling" with others. 5

"W.E." is Your Key to Success

W.E. is success! It is about putting your skills to work to make personal strides, individual performance better, customer service better, and the company better. It's about improving your bottom line because everyone is on board with what the goal is, what is expected of them, and where you are heading. It's about being better than your competition! It's profitability!

W.E. is a mindset. It is a way of life. It is a feeling deep down inside you that tells you to . . . "try again, try harder and don't give up!" W.E. compels you to get up every day and makes you ready to face the challenges of that day. More precisely, W.E. is that driving force that keeps after you to . . . "stay at it—you know you can do it!" W.E. feels exhilarating, motivating and exciting.

W.E. is a foundation—it's your roots! It is also your inspiration. W.E. represents your compassion, consideration and understanding. When you have faith and trust in yourself, you can achieve anything. A solid work ethic can bring you all the best things in life because you have earned them.

W.E. is also a choice, and it is up to you to choose a solid work ethic. W.E. is full of possibilities and it only takes your imagination to make things happen. It may surprise you to discover that you never really know what you are capable of until you try. So, get out there and Be Smart. Make WE your key. A solid work ethic is your key to success. In the end, it all comes down to WE!

Outlining the
Five Components of "W.E."
1. How to focus.

Goals will aid your efforts to focus.

In order to succeed with "W.E.," you need to have the desire to make changes in your life; a key strategy for success with building a work ethic is to set goals. First, set a goal in your mind. Decide what you want and need to do. Then determine your plan for getting there. Here are a few key steps for setting realistic, timely goals and finally achieving your dreams.

Goal setting.

1. Determine what you want to achieve and when. Set realistic time frames.
2. Focus all your efforts on accomplishing your goal(s).
3. Establish milestones to strive for and then assign dates.
4. Evaluate your progress periodically.
5. Celebrate reaching your goals!

Not everyone will have the same goals with W.E. If you are good at focusing but poor at follow-through, set a goal to achieve follow-through as part of your overall plan. Don't be afraid to adjust your goals or the deadlines associated with them. That does not mean failure, it means you are attune to and active with your goals. Don't forget that some of life's distractions may affect the outcome from time to time, but do not let them deter you from your goal. Therefore, our first component, Focus, is an essential aspect of work ethic.

Focus.

- Watches, listens and learns.
- Able to stay on task. Does what is expected.

- Identifies what must be done and completes the job.
- Follows instructions/directions. Pays attention to their work.

You need to "be present" or focused to have a good W.E. That means you must be able to put all else aside. When we come to work with distractions we do no one any good, not the customer, our boss, nor ourselves. Here are ways to stay focused.

Watches, listens and learns.

Keep your eyes, mind and ears open to the directions you are given so you can focus. To do this, you always need to listen well so you can follow instructions accurately. Listening effectively can be a challenge to many of us. When you listen, you can do your work without asking numerous questions or taking far too long to complete a task.

I was once a poor listener myself. I can remember a scenario years ago, when I was asked to deliver a package to a department head at the manufacturing company where I worked at the time. This package had important and timely information in it for a negotiations process that was currently going on. I thought I listened to the instructions regarding the delivery of the package to the executive who worked at a different location from where I worked, but I must have failed to grasp the urgency and need for delivery by a 1:00 p.m. deadline. It was about 11:45 a.m. when I left the plant with the package, and I headed out to find some lunch and enjoy some free time away from my desk. I proceeded to stop at a local dress shop and browse for about 30 minutes looking at clothing that I wanted to buy. Then I drove to a deli and ordered a sandwich and drink, and proceeded to watch a baseball game on their TV as I ate. It is important to remember that we did not have cellular phones, so I could not be reached by anyone at any time. I sat and ate lunch for about 45 minutes and enjoyed the game and just relaxing. About the time I was ready to leave the deli it was about 1:15 p.m. I sauntered out to my car and drove about 15 minutes to the other plant. Upon my casual arrival

I was greeted by an anxious receptionist and shortly thereafter by an angry department head who was very agitated by the fact that his meeting and subsequent documents for presentation were late and soon to be disregarded. Needless to say, I was reprimanded and nearly lost my job due to my lack of attention and sense of urgency.

From that point forward, I began a conscientious process of listening closely and taking notes when assigned tasks and projects in my work.

It might seem that listening is an obvious skill. One that can be achieved without effort. However, the true art of listening involves more than just your ears. It involves engaging your mind to ensure comprehension of the content of the message. Solid listening skills can be achieved with a few basic steps. Here are some useful tips for becoming a better listener.

The Art of Listening

Learning how to listen effectively can be one of the most powerful skills anyone can master. Solid listening skills will help you communicate more effectively and solve more problems.

1. **Keep a neat, clean area, especially when meeting with others.** Clutter sends the message of disorganization. You may also tend to fiddle with things instead of paying attention to your guest. Set work aside when someone comes to talk.
2. **Notice something special about each person.** Make a concerted effort to look at the color of your guest's eyes, hair style, or other safe attribute. Noticing a feature like eye color helps you focus in on that person and what they are saying. Memory of that feature may help you recall information or tie a discussion to them, increasing your effectiveness.
3. **Put your thoughts in the form of a question, and listen to the response.** Instead of constantly saying . . . "Did you get that done?" use a more constructive approach such as, "how's that job coming along?" Ask questions to find out more—don't

assume that things are a certain way. Then listen to their response.

4. **Mind your manners.** Be respectful at all times. Use common courtesies as well as phrases of understanding and acknowledgement. "Yes, I understand" or "I see what you mean" goes a lot further than . . . "you are not clear" or "you did not think that through."

5. **Opening your ears, can open up possibilities.** You don't have to have all the answers. Sometimes saying . . . "what would you think we could do about that?" works very well. Listen to the individual's ideas and thoughts, and add yours (. . ."what about?") after discussing theirs.

6. **Be present. Pay attention.** Don't let your mind wander off to other tasks or matters. Keep focused on the person and their conversation. Keep in mind how it feels to be "tuned out" and pledge never to do it yourself.

Able to stay on task. Does what is expected.

Next, stay on task. That means you start and then finish the work as assigned or required. You need to be able to focus on what needs to be done, do it as expected, and complete the work entirely.

For example, if you are filling an order at McDonald's®, you have to make sure the entire order is complete before you give it to the customer. That completed work may include the fries, sandwich and drink. You may also have to collect their money and make sure you provide the proper change. What is important is that you are present in your day, focus on the task at hand, and do what is expected to complete the entire job. Remember, you are working for this company, and you must do what is expected to keep your job.

Identify what must be done and complete the job.

An effective individual will determine what needs to be done and develop a plan for completing the work. If written steps or a plan for completing the work is not provided, prepare one of your own. Keep your notes close at hand while doing your work. Most bosses will appreciate the initiative when they see you are using notes or steps to ensure a complete job. Never think it is silly or amateur to work from a plan. The best minds in history worked from a plan for what they wanted to achieve. Be one of those great minds. Thorough planning and foresight provides the structure for your success.

Finally, determine—in your mind—the best way to complete the job, then do it. As I said, if you are better at writing things down, then by all means, write the steps down. Know in what order work must be done to achieve the final outcome and then "stay the course" until the job is done.

Follow instructions/directions. Pay attention to your work.

Finally, follow the instructions and directions provided to you. These steps are provided for a reason and many times the reason may not become apparent until later when you have learned all aspects of your work.

You must pay attention to what you are doing at all times in order to be successful. Keep the important steps and instructions in mind (or on paper) when you are working. If you focus on the goal, the work does not seem so tedious. It should be your goal to provide a good product or service, one that has value and is considered worthwhile.

> **"WE" Capsule:** Make sure your W.E. efforts always stay
> grounded in the foundational beliefs of respect,
> fairness and ethical treatment for all individuals.
> It is key to your success!

Five Components of "W.E."
2. Don't quit. Never give up your dreams.

To develop a good work ethic you must never give up your dreams. Dreams (goals) are those things that we deem most important to our happiness. These goals do not have to be lofty ones, but they must be yours (things you value). Let's look at some examples of what your dreams might look like.

Some potential Dreams (goals):

- Be a singer or musician
- Be an artist
- Be a school teacher
- Be a nurse or doctor
- Be a mom
- Be happy and contented

To reach your dreams you must have a "stick to it" attitude. You must believe that you can achieve them, in your heart and soul, and then you must go after those dreams with a vengeance. Let's take a look at the next component of W.E. and the characteristics of someone who doesn't quit.

Doesn't quit.

- Learns from mistakes. Keeps going even against adversity.
- Stays the course. Keeps trying.
- Doesn't give up. Not a quitter.
- Doesn't let challenges distract them.

Learns from mistakes. Keeps going even against adversity.

One of the bigger challenges to changing your work ethic is to not fall back into old, bad habits. You have to really want to change your life. In my lifetime I have repeatedly experienced that I was most satisfied and proud when I acquired a skill or learned something new. Many times this learning occurred as a result of a difficult or adverse situation.

I want to share with you a couple of poignant stories that helped me grow from these experiences.

Agent of Change. As I mentioned earlier, I had a job—actually, my first real job—working in a travel agency in downtown Chicago. I was young and naive, but looking forward to learning and growing in this job. My role at this company was to be the receptionist to the offices as well as a travel agent. I accepted it willingly and did my best to learn the value of customer service, answering phones, and booking travel for our customers. I spent the better part of two years learning the ropes at this agency. I almost threw it all away one day because of my carelessness and lack of focus.

One of my supervisors at this travel agency was Barbara and she had given me the day's receipts (about $4,000) in a pouch to take to the bank in our building a couple of floors below. I was so glad to get out of the office, so I grabbed the pouch and hurried out of the office. As I mentioned, I was young and scatterbrained, and had decided to stop at the restroom on the same floor as the bank to fix my hair and put on some lipstick. I became distracted talking to others in the bathroom about fashion, makeup, etc. and walked out of the restroom talking casually with another girl— without the pouch. Not thinking about what I was doing, I said goodbye to my friend and hopped on the elevator to return to my office. I didn't realize that I had just made a huge mistake by not paying attention to what I was doing.

No sooner had the elevator door closed and we started to move, I realized what I had done. I immediately started to panic. I punched at the elevator floor buttons in haste, but this elevator was on its way up to several higher floors. I jumped out at the next floor, pushed the down button and rushed onto the next elevator going down. I don't think that even three minutes had passed at this point. When the elevator stopped back at the bank floor, I rushed out and into the restroom to see if I could find the pouch. As I had feared, it was gone. I knew that the money from the pouch was now in somebody's pocket. Fear set in and I was beside myself with anxiety about the repercussions. What was I going to say to my boss, Barbara? Would I lose my job? Will she take the entire value of the pouch out of my next few paychecks?

As I rode solemnly back up to the floor of my offices, I was searching my mind for a story I could give that would explain my careless actions. I finally, and rightfully, decided to tell the truth about leaving the pouch in the restroom. I knew that the best story was the truth, and I would have to be prepared to deal with the consequences. As I approached my boss Barbara to tell her what had happened, she noticed the look of anguish on my face and asked what was the matter. Before I could respond, she teased me by asking coyly if I had lost anything lately. I looked at her with a puzzled look, and she proceeded to tell me that she had just received a call from a manager at the bank who told her that a teller had found and retrieved our deposit pouch in the bathroom and made our deposit. The bank manager wanted to make sure that we knew right away that the money had been found and they had saved the day. I was embarrassed but never so relieved in all my life.

I learned an important lesson that day: pay attention to the task at hand. If I hadn't been so distracted and immature, I'd have never been so careless. I remember this valuable lesson every day so I don't repeat it.

How your work ethic can help you grow and learn.

Here are a few W.E. quotations that have helped me and may help you on your way to becoming a happier, healthier, and more successful person.

- Work ethic builds character.
- Work ethic instills pride.
- Work ethic is ever changing and improving.
- Work ethic is an achievement of which to be prou.
- Work ethic is a foundation for more solid characteristics.
- Work ethic is knowing and doing the right thing.
- Work ethic is carrying your own weight.

- Work ethic is pride.
- Work ethic is people-oriented.
- Work ethic is the roadway to happiness.
- Work ethic is in each of us—waiting to be born, discovered and unearthed.
- Work ethic is learning.
- Work ethic means "never having to say you're sorry."
- Work ethic means achievement.
- Work ethic means ownership.
- Work ethic mean happiness.
- Work ethic means going the long haul.
- Work ethic means sticking to it no matter the adversity.

Choose one or two of these quotations for your own personal inspiration and post them where you can see and read them every day.

Stays the course. Keeps trying.

What does it mean to "stay the course?" If more people would stay the course, we'd have a lot less failures in customer service and a better work environment. Why? Because jobs would be done in their entirety and with accuracy.

Here are some steps for "staying the course:"

1. Finish what you start.
2. Don't be distracted.
3. Keep trying until you succeed.
4. Do what is expected.
5. Follow through until the work is done.

These are pointers for staying on track with your work and your life's goals and dreams.

Doesn't give up. Not a quitter.

The challenge of changing the way you work, think and see your future doesn't need to be a daunting one. It all is in how you look at it. You have probably done other challenging things in your life such as lose some weight, make a career change, or end a relationship, and you know as well as I do that it's all in how you look at the task that makes all the difference. Half the fun of implementing your new W.E. is discovering what you are capable of. Figuring out how far you can go and what you can achieve is invigorating. Use the following characteristics to continue your efforts:

1. Have stamina.
2. Persevere.
3. Focus your thoughts/efforts.
4. Keep on track.

Stamina is essential. Work ethic is very much about keeping going against adversity. Remind yourself, as necessary, about what you are striving to achieve and go forward.

Perseverance is important as well. Stay the course even when challenges arise. Your ability to focus will aid you at this time. When you become frustrated with your progress or those day-to-day challenges that can distract you, remember to focus your thoughts.

Finally, keeping on track and making progress, regardless of how little, will help you to avoid the quitter mentality or the desire to give up. You have to look at every step forward as progress, no matter how small, and have confidence that you can reach your intended goal. Implementing these types of efforts will help you to manage your goals more easily and to allow for a gradual change in your thinking about your work ethic obstacles.

Don't let challenges distract you.

As you traverse the road of life and make the journey into W.E. territory, be careful to keep your friends at hand and your enemies at arm's length. There will always be those who will try to bring you down, distract you or just plain waste your time. But as you know, the world is made up of many kinds of people, good and bad, and your challenge is to rise above, learn from, and focus efforts on goals and dreams.

Here are some easy steps for dealing with the challenge of distractions:

1. Define what you want to achieve/change/accomplish. Be specific.
2. Set a reasonable time frame for change. Set some milestone dates.
3. Be flexible when you encounter a difficulty or set-back. Change your dates.
4. Be a problem solver—come up with solutions. Do not be detered.
5. Keep your goal out in front of you at all times! Post it everywhere as a reminder.
6. Remember to have fun with the process. Keep a positive mindset about learning.

Your W.E. goals and dreams in life may best be reached through attention to detail and focused efforts. If you learned to stay focused early in life, you are lucky. It has become a part of who you are. If you did not, you may have a tougher road—but still an achievable one—in learning the fine art of a good work ethic.

My first job in human resources was working in a steel manufacturing plant on the northwest side of Chicago back in the late 70s and early 80s. This plant was a rough environment, and the steelworkers who worked in the plant were a tough group. I was a young and naive professional, just starting out in human resources, and I had much to learn. I was tasked with handling grievance investigations at this plant. That meant I had to go out onto the shop floor and talk with union workers about complaints and gather information about work conditions and situations. Many times, while on the floor, I would be pinched, whistled at, or teased by the male workers because I was young, inexperienced and pretty. I am sure I must have seemed like a dolt to them; a bit green. I recall one time in particular walking into a labor meeting with my boss and hearing muffled cat calls and whistles from the union workers outside as I walked to the table to be seated. There were even sexist comments made to my face such as "What are you doing after work Sweetie?" and my face would always flush a bright red in color.

I can tell you that inside I was terrified and embarrassed. I was afraid that they would know, too. But my boss, Joe, was a sharp guy, and he looked out for me and kept those wolves at arm's length. He would focus on the task at hand, make sure that I was included, and teach me what was going on and how the labor process worked. Later, away from the meeting, he would talk to me at length about the role of our team, the history of the plant, and the nuances of the labor negotiations process. I learned so much and respected him for his patience and willingness to share these insights. To this very day, he is an inspiration as well as a valuable story that I relate when teaching my workshop attendees about the value of patience, communication, and employee relations.

"WE" Capsule: Make sure your W.E. efforts always stay
grounded in the foundational beliefs of respect,
fairness and ethical treatment for all individuals.
It is key to your success!

Five Components of "W.E."
3. Shares and Bears the Work Load.

The biggest sense of accomplishment in life is to look back at what you've done and enjoy the pride of having achieved it. I believe that our soul needs this kind of nourishment—that without it, we tend to feel unfulfilled, and may even waiver in our efforts. True satisfaction stems from being a part of a successful team, project or work effort.

Many of us thrive on the sense of contribution and sharing, and we need to feel a part of or in on things. That is where the next component: share the load, stems from, our need for belonging.

Shares and bears the work load.

- A good team player. Doesn't make excuses.
- Carries and completes their share of the work and then some.
- Be present at your job.
- Pitches in without hesitation. Makes a contribution.

A good team player. Don't make excuses.

A good team player is willing and able to do whatever is required of them to help the team reach success. That means pitching in and doing your fair share of the workload. Here are some ways to build your team strength:

- Think "help your team."
- Make no excuses.
- Carry your own weight.

Do not worry about the amount of work that someone else is doing at the time, just forge ahead and complete your work as assigned; when or if someone is not pulling their weight or completing their share of the work, it will be revealed in the end.

Those types of lazy workers do not go unnoticed, however, those who constantly focus on the flaws and short-comings of others, tend to be seen as weak and spiteful. The non-performers will be weeded out over time because their impact will be felt by the entire team and have a noticeable drain on productivity.

Completes their share of the work and then some.

Always be aware of your role on the team. There is no honor in slacking off or in living by the motto that "whatever I don't do, someone else will catch on the next shift." You need to be accountable for your job, your role, and completing all of the work assigned to you without hesitation. If possible, do a little more—go above and beyond. When you cover for other co-workers, especially those who are overwhelmed or just learning the ropes, you help them to feel a valued part of your team. Once they get up to speed, they will be more likely to help you out in return when you need it.

Be present at your job.

When you "sign in"—stay in mentally. With W.E. it is important to stay engaged, think ahead, keep your eyes open, pay attention to details, focus on the customer, and be aware of your fellow team members. Again, let's repeat the ways we stay present:

- Stay engaged.
- Think ahead.
- Keep your eyes open.
- Pay attention to details.
- Focus on the customer.
- Be aware of your team members.

For example, if you were working in a construction job, and your coworker kept forgetting to put the safety switch on when their nail gun was not in use, wouldn't you be cautious around him or her? Might you wonder when or if you were going to get "nailed?" Sure you would. So why is it ok to slack off in whatever job you do? It never is! Always pay attention and be present at your job so that you can earn your wage, do your fair share, and leave work with a clear conscience each and every day.

Pitches in without hesitation. Makes a contribution.

When you "share the work load" you are making a valuable contribution to the efforts of your team or crew. Don't think no one will notice if you don't do your share—they do. And in most cases they resent it. But if you are making an effort, being a contributor is more valuable than you know to your future and your self esteem. Contribution is an essential characteristic for reaching personal satisfaction and overall well being. It has its foundations in our basic psychology of well being, such as how we perceive ourselves, our self esteem, and in how we feel valued by those around us. To make a contribution you must:

- Go for it.
- Try a new strategy.
- Contribute freely.

By pitching in, especially without hesitation, you will be remembered for your willingness to ensure team success. This behavior also allows you to experience all aspects of the work being performed and broadens your experiences and horizons. Go ahead and pitch in with enthusiasm and zeal, and you will learn more about yourself. You may find that you receive more attention at work which may translate into new opportunities for advancement due to your contributing nature.

One of the guys my husband worked with in construction used to slack off on his duties and go hide in a corner somewhere and sleep. He figured there were plenty of others to do the work and cover for him and that a few minutes of sleep "really shouldn't matter, right?" It didn't take long for the others on the crew to realize he was "missing" and they began to resent his laziness and lack of concern about it. Eventually he was found out and lost his job.

People will only put up with poor efforts in special cases and usually temporarily, if they know that the person is struggling, learning or in poor health. But in most work crews, everyone who is able-bodied is expected to pull their own weight. There is little sympathy for those who choose not to contribute.

This foundational component of W.E., share the workload, was one of the more essential aspects of our family philosophy. On our farm, there was always another task waiting to be done, and we knew that when we worked together, each task would go more easily, more quickly, and with less effort required on the part of each individual.

I still adhere to this philosophy today as I approach any work situation. I find myself frustrated when others do not care about or comprehend the needs of others when working. I guess you could say I believe it should be inherent in each of us, from birth, to activate an understanding and compassion for our fellow man at each and every opportunity. It is my goal, through this book, to awaken, instill or invigorate this essential understanding and passion for our work ethic and to help us rise above our petty differences, ways of treating or thinking about the welfare of another.

Are you able to work well with others?

One of the secrets of W.E. is to be able to work with others and build or support something (a goal) that is bigger and more important than you. The synergy of a strong team can do amazing things when everyone is on the same page and has the same focus.

To know if you can work well with others, ask yourself the following questions.

1. Are you able to find happiness in shared success? Yes No
2. Do you need to be the center of attention? Yes No

3. Can you work with others toward a common goal?	Yes	No
4. Do you understand the bigger picture and your role in achieving it?	Yes	No

If you answered "yes" to three out of the four questions, you are on your way to being a solid team player. However, a "yes" to one question above may lead to problems with others and a need for more credit than you deserve. Which question above do you think W.E. are talking about?

Someone who works well with others will listen to direction, take their role seriously, and value the efforts of others they work with. They do not have to get all the credit or the spotlight focused on them, and they understand that most things worth achieving at work are done with and through others. Being a part of a team has its rewards as well:

- You can achieve more with others than you can alone.
- You can share in the credit for great achievements that may not have been reached otherwise.
- You have a sense of family and belonging with a team as opposed to isolation.

Remember that there is an important expression that fits here: There is no "I" in team.

"Watch for a Sign"

One guy I worked with was at the top of the food chain in his company. He was the president of this company, and he was a good person. Now, normally those two characteristics don't go hand in hand, but this guy was different. He had a natural way with all employees, and they liked him quite well for it. He was always approachable at work and made sure his regime included the requirement that all the managers and supervisors make themselves available for their employees. In that way, no one in his company would feel as though they didn't have input.

Well, the company was growing and expanding those days. One day, they made an important decision to put a new, larger-than-life sign out front of their building—it would be bigger than any of the competition. It was an expensive endeavor, so approvals were obtained and the sign was ordered and installed. It towered over the street and was amazing and colorful. One night a terrible storm hit the city with high winds and heavy rain and the sign did not hold up against this weather. It came tumbling down onto the street, luckily not hurting anyone, but making a huge mess. As it turned out, someone had to be held accountable, and this guy was the one. Fingers had to be pointed at someone for making the decision on that sign. Now, you may be thinking as I did, why would this guy lose his job when he did not build or install the defective sign? Well, there was a mindset that someone had to be held accountable for mistakes, and this guy was the one, regardless of his track record for success up to that point.

This company proceeded to have several successors in this high level position over the coming years, but no one was ever able to live up to the sheer quality, sincerity and goodness of the man who gave us a sign.

"WE" Capsule: Make sure your W.E. efforts always stay
grounded in the foundational beliefs of respect,
fairness and ethical treatment for all individuals.
It is key to your success!

Five Components of "W.E."
4. Finishes the Job.

So much of the gap between effort and good intentions lies with the inability to follow through with a job to its completion. Yes—until it is totally finished! I blame the existence of this work ethic gap on the lack of accountability in so many individuals. This is how we have gotten into the mess we are facing today. Many people today have never learned to nor were they ever held accountable for completing a single chore, task or any continued effort—NOT A SINGLE THING?!

What do you get when individuals are not held to a standard or do not learn to be accountable? At best you get marginal efforts and results. You get half-finished tasks and work. You get poor service and even poorer attitudes. I often hear . . . "Oh, well, that's the best I can do!" What kind of excuse is that for poor work efforts? I can tell you this, that is not "follow through."

Outlined below is the fourth component of W.E. and a few ways to help you to develop follow through and finish your work completely.

Finishes the job.

- Does all as expected. Embraces the value of follow through.
- Completes all aspects of their work.
- No half-way work. Finishes up.
- Doesn't leave work or trash behind for others. Cleans up.

Does all as expected. Embraces the value of follow through.

The first step in ensuring good follow through is to recognize that all the aspects of a job need to be completed before the job is done. Those aspects include, in order: job description (work to be done), work process (steps to completing a job), and work completion (conclusion of work, clean up and acknowledgement). Here are those aspects:

- Job description (work to be done)
  - o Description or details of all that needs to be done to complete a job.
  - o Outlines skills, processes and job requirements.

A job description should include the essential functions and tasks for a job. It should outline the skills, knowledge, and experience necessary to complete the work.

- Work process (steps to completing a job)
  - o Steps necessary to do or complete the work associated with a job.
  - o Ability to grasp the steps associated with completing work.

A good work process should outline all the steps necessary for the completion of a job or task. These should be outlined in order of priority for completion of each task or step. The individual assigned to the work must have the qualifications to do the work which enables them to understand the work process without difficulty.

- Work completion (conclusion of work, clean up and acknowledgement)
  - o Fulfilling the job requirements by taking action to complete work.
  - o Recognition that all aspects of a job must be completed for closure.

The most important step in follow through is completion of the work. Once the work is undertaken, it is essential that all steps are completed. Each individual on the job must actively work to meet the expectations, follow through on all tasks, and communicate the status of their work to the next crew, shift or person doing this work. If you work independently, you must note where you left off so that you can effectively start at that point on your next work day.

Completes all aspects of a job.

There are several important but simple steps to implementing your plan to make sure you complete all aspects of your work.

- Make note of what needs to happen and when. (job process)
- Commit work process to memory or paper (records it).
- Value each important step—each are essential to reaching your goal.
- Think to yourself . . . "finish what I started."

For example, if you find a bolt left over at the end of the assembly of your "widget," isn't your work faulty or incomplete? The essence of this W.E. step is "all aspects." There is far too much justifying today that "the next guy/gal can finish up where I left off."

Every time we undertake work, we must think accountability. We take on a responsibility when we work and we must have the integrity to finish the work assigned.

No half-way work. finishes up.

Conscientious persons will "finish up" all their work and leave the work area ready for those who follow. But finishing up has a more comprehensive meaning than just neatness. It has a psychological meaning for us as well. When completing your day's work, a task or a project, ask yourself these kinds of questions:

- Have I done all that is expected of me for this job, task or day?
- Was my work a quality effort?
- Have I kept my crew or company informed of my progress or the status of my work?
- What must I do to ensure a thorough and safe follow through at all times?

Finishing up involves organizing and communicating our thoughts about what was and needs to be done. We evaluate these thoughts in our mind to understand our role, belonging and contribution to the workplace and those around us. It also involves grasping the value of our contribution and being proud of it.

It is ultimately important that we view or embrace our work efforts as important and significant contributions. What we do in our jobs does influence and impact others, whether it be overall service, safety concerns, or accuracy in assembly. It is our conscious awareness of this role and our contribution that ensures a good job. We must embrace and acknowledge our value, and if we do, we can develop pride in our accomplishments and our contributions.

Doesn't leave work or trash behind for others. Cleans up.

This aspect may seem trivial or nit-picky to some, however it is far more important than it would appear on the surface. Leaving incomplete work is not only careless but it means your work is unfinished and shoddy. When you do a "half-way" job at something, including not cleaning up, what does that say about you? It says you don't care enough about your results to ensure your final work product looks as is expected. Let me express my point with a couple of simple examples.

Q. If you dress for a formal occasion—take a shower, fix your hair and brush your teeth—but your clothing has a terrible stain or looks messy or unkempt, what is the impression people will have of you?

A. They may think you are sloppy or do not care about your appearance.

- Regardless of the reality of your efforts, you are perceived as messy, sloppy, etc.

Q. If you work hard completing a report, as directed by your boss, but the final copy is smudged with coffee stains, wrinkled or

Linda Westcott-Bernstein

torn, or your figures don't add up, what does your boss see
when you give the report to him/her?
A. He/she will only see the errors and mess, and is not impressed
with your results.
• Regardless of the reality of your efforts, you are perceived as
messy, sloppy, etc.
Q. If you are hired to paint a room, but fail to ensure consistent
coverage, spill paint on the floor, and leave the window sills
and door jams with splotches of paint left over from the
painting process, what is the impression of your customer?
A. They may feel that you do poor quality work, tell others about
your poor work, and/or refuse to pay you.
• Regardless of the reality of your efforts, you are perceived as
messy, sloppy, etc.

These examples reflect the reality about perception more than
most of us would care to admit.

None of these outcomes are good ones nor are they something
to be taken lightly. They reflect a carelessness or cavalier attitude
about your work. In many cases, individuals may struggle with
this part in the work ethic process, thinking that the completion
of the work is enough. But, it is up to you to decide who and
what you want to be remembered for and how you want to be
perceived. You are always making choices in your life about your
work product as well as the impression you make with others. It
may be time to clean up your act.

> **"WE" Capsule:** Make sure your W.E. efforts always stay
> grounded in the foundational beliefs of respect, fairness and
> ethical treatment for all individuals. It is key to your
> success!

Five Components of "W.E."
5. Take pride in a job well done.

Last, but not least, is the final component of W.E.: taking pride in your accomplishments. What good is work ethic if you can't or don't enjoy your successes? And, in my opinion, the most important outcome of building a new way of thinking is enjoying the way you feel when you achieve success.

One of the most effective ways to keep W.E. alive is to recognize the achievements, milestones and growth of those who embrace it. What effort, left unrewarded, ever continues? What changes in performance, if not celebrated, continue to occur in individuals? Not too many that I have experienced. We all desire some level of recognition.

Let's discuss the various components of exhibiting W.E. pride.

Exhibits pride.

- Appears self-confident and self-assured.
- Performs job with superior effort.
- Genuinely proud of successes.
- Shares the "good feeling" with others.

Appears self-confident and self-assured.

Anyone who has achieved success shares a commonality with all others who have been successful. It is an exhilarating sense of confidence and a feeling of self assurance. These psychological rewards keep us striving for more in life. What are some ways for embracing the true value of confidence?

1. Bask in the good feeling of achievement.
2. Allow pride to seep into and fill you.
3. Recognize that confidence is good for your heart and soul.

When we achieve our goals or accomplish even basic levels of self-improvement, our confidence grows and helps us become more self-assured. What is self assurance?

- Belief in your value.
- Faith in yourself and your worth.
- The ability to continue to strive for more.

Self assurance provides us with the motivation for doing more and going further in life.

Performs job with superior effort.

It is evident that those who have pride in their work make a more concerted effort to do their jobs well. They have learned the value of the good feeling that comes from their achievements, contributions and good efforts. What does a superior effort look like?

1. Does the work to the best of their ability.
2. Takes the time to accurately complete all the work.
3. Engages their mind on their work.
4. Recognizes that their work affects others.

Anyone can apply these efforts but you must have the desire to make positive changes in your life and future. You have to want to give more than 100% effort when doing your work and you must be ok with the effort required to make that outcome happen.

Genuinely proud of successes.

So much of our societal conditioning tells us to be modest or self-depreciating because to be otherwise is to be arrogant. I am telling you that is baloney! It is ok to be proud of your efforts and successes! I have found that pride in my accomplishments has acted like a fuel for much of my ongoing efforts. Here is some fuel to help you achieve more:

- Smile outwardly and inwardly.
- Accept accolades graciously.
- Walk with confidence.
- Allow yourself to be an expert or authority.
- Let others know of your deeds.
- Enjoy the notoriety.
- Confidence is good for the heart, soul and mind.

It is these "fuels" that drive your desire for more success, more effort, more recognition, and more out of life. I am not talking about being boastful or arrogant. Genuine pride is neither of those but is truly good for us!

Shares the "good feeling" with others.

When you have mastered your ability to be comfortable with the "good feeling" of achievement, then you can spread it beyond yourself and get out the word to others.

- Share with others "how you did it."
- Allow others to "share" in your experience(s).
- Sincerely want good outcomes for others.

When you are a positive influence on those around you, they can sense your strength and will want to share in what you are experiencing. Everyone wants to feel good! Deep down inside, I believe that everyone wants to be adored, appreciated and valued. These are basic human needs. What are your basic needs?

• Active life	• Love
• Awareness	• Matrimony
• Achievement	• Partnership
• Belonging	• Recognition
• Engagement	• Sharing
• Excitement	• Tolerance
• Faith	• Understanding

- Family
- Involvement
- Worth
- Yellow (ok, it's my favorite color)

In Maslow's hierarchy of needs, once basic requirements for food and shelter are met, we seek more out of life and want to go to the next level of our needs. Amidst his process of evolution is a need for belonging and acceptance. Can we achieve acceptance by doing our fair share, by making our contribution, and by implementing a solid work ethic? It is possible. It is all up to you.

For each of us, our goals and desires in life differ. But our satisfaction lies in doing those things that bring us pride, joy and sense of worth. You may have to honestly and openly assess what you desire in life and then reach for it. There is nothing holding you back but you!

And remember, success is contagious! So go ahead . . . embrace the good feeling and share it with everyone around you.

"WE" Capsule: Make sure your W.E. efforts always stay grounded in the foundational beliefs of respect, fairness and ethical treatment for all individuals. It is key to your success!

CHAPTER 5

Driving Home "W.E."
How you drive "W.E." momentum

When I was a child, I would listen while my parents told stories about how the work they had done in life had contributed in one way or another to where they were today. They understood that by repeating those stories to us and showing good work behaviors, over time those examples would influence our behaviors and make an impression on us which would stay in our minds.

W.E. may be the most impactful effort you will ever undertake if you allow it to be present in all aspects of your life. To drive your success, you need to completely immerse yourself in W.E. thinking, W.E. behaviors, W.E. standards and W.E. outcomes.

The best way to gain momentum is to jump in with both feet. When you are ready to make a change in your life with W.E., it is best to take an all or nothing approach just like you would to stop smoking. Only then, when you are ready, willing and able for W.E., can you learn a W.E. way of thinking which will enable you to change your life for the better.

Here is some helpful advice for taking the plunge and for driving W.E. momentum . . .

- Watch for and exhibit W.E. behaviors (at all times).
- Set clear W.E. expectations.
- Implement W.E. standards.
- Assess engagement against W.E. standards & expectations.

Watch for and exhibit W.E. behaviors.

Some of you already have sound work ethic behaviors. If you do, that means you may already have the right mindset of "focus and follow through." You may also have a support network of individuals who share your beliefs. That is an important first step! These focused people and efforts will help you reach success. They can help build this new work ethic foundation that you want to achieve. Use your talents and theirs to effect change. Have them be your Diplomats (see Page 111) of change. Allow them to be your eyes and ears throughout the process.

When striving for an effective W.E. environment you must watch for and support W.E. behaviors. The following are some behaviors which exhibit W.E. efforts. They should be recognized and applauded, as often as possible.

- Going the extra mile—doing more than expected!
- Hard work has noticeable results—give out kudos!
- People supporting one another—let it be known!
- Completing a big project—celebrate your success!
- Apparent changes in attitudes toward work—share the workload!

The best way to ensure success at any endeavor is to watch for and recognize efforts being made toward the goal, everyone has something to contribute. Keep your mind and your door open: which says, "I want to hear what you have to say." or "I want to share what I know." When you reach a milestone, celebrate the accomplishment!

Set clear W.E. expectations.

When implementing the W.E. components (see Chapter 4), do so consistently and clearly. Again, here are those five essential components.

1. Focus on the job at hand.
2. Don't give up or quit.
3. Share and bear the load.
4. Finish the job—completely.
5. Take pride in a job well done.

You have some flexibility in the actual wording, but the five basic components of any W.E. Standards should be fairly consistent.

Make sure you are clear about the expectations. Everyone should be on the same page regarding what is expected and what performance criteria you are watching for. When all is clearly communicated and understood, you are likely to have more and better success. Here's how you can help to ensure you are on the right track:

- Share W.E. expectations openly.
- Keep all expectations simple, clear and straight forward.
- Include W.E. expectations in your job descriptions.
- Communicate W.E. progress in all your correspondence.
- Train your staff, especially your new hires, on W.E. expectations.

For work ethic momentum, I encourage you to be original and flexible in your efforts. Try some new approaches to your implementation—keep things fresh and new. You could try some of these ideas.

- W.E. standard of the week.
- W.E. idea of the month.
- W.E. Diplomat's choice.
- W.E. team of the quarter.

Incorporate the concepts and beliefs that identify and support your culture, and pepper in those concepts that are present in your W.E. initiative.

Implement W.E. standards.

The W.E. Standards, also outlined in Chapter 4, are the benchmarks against which the performance and success of your efforts will be measured. No ambiguity. Just clear, concise standards from which to assess your performance.

The first, and foremost standard, is the ability to focus your efforts on the work at hand and your goals.

1. *Focus.*
   - *Watches, listens and learns.*
   - *Able to stay on task. Does what is expected.*
   - *Identifies what must be done and completes the job.*
   - *Follows instructions/directions. Pays attention to their work.*

Establish the traits of focus, attention to detail, staying on task, ability to listen, and ability to follow through as well as ability to implement a plan for completing work. Everyone must engage his/her mind for success at learning. The above focus expectations are all sound methods for evaluation of strong focus, the initial component of work ethic.

The next standard, is the trait of "sticking with it" or not quitting, or having a "stay with it" attitude.

2. *Doesn't quit.*
   - *Learns from mistakes. Keeps going even against adversity.*
   - *Stays the course. Keeps trying.*
   - *Doesn't give up. Not a quitter.*
   - *Doesn't let challenges distract them.*

Assess staying power. The essence of a solid work ethic is your ability to stay the course and not give up or quit. Additionally, with W.E., individuals will want to learn—not just rely on asking questions for answers. That means you have to engage your mind, follow through, and have staying power for success.

The third standard is the ability to pitch in and share the work load with others as necessary.

3. **Shares and bears the work load.**
    - **A good team player. Doesn't make excuses.**
    - **Carries and completes his/her share of the work and then some.**
    - **Be present at your job.**
    - **Pitches in without hesitation. Makes a contribution.**

For this component, each individual must find what they value in teamwork and feel satisfaction in being a team player. We must feel a sense of obligation to support the team and readily carry our share of the work load. It is essential for each individual to engage their mind on behalf of the team in order to embrace commitment and to feel the reward of contribution. The premise . . . "we can accomplish more as a team than individually" holds true and is a solid W.E. concept.

The next standard is the expectation that all work will be completed in its entirety to finish the job.

4. **Finishes the job.**
    - **Does all as expected. Embraces the value of follow through.**
    - **Completes all aspects of his/her work.**
    - **No half-way work. Finishes up.**
    - **Doesn't leave work or trash behind for others. Cleans up.**

The completion of a job, in its entirety, is one of the underlying key aspects of having a good work ethic. No job is complete until all aspects, including follow—through, occurs. Follow-through involves communication of the status of a job and any potential concerns associated with a job to those continuing the effort. Finishing a job shows pride, reflects consideration and embodies a conscientious effort to consider the others associated with the work. It is also important to never leave work behind for others, including clean up of your work area, tools, and such.

In order to appreciate the value of finishing a job completely, individuals must engage their minds and embrace the importance of team when contributing to the goal.

Finally, to retain overall momentum in the W.E. process, you must show pride in your work and enjoy the rewards of accomplishment.

5. **Exhibits pride.**
   - *Appears self-confident and self-assured.*
   - *Performs job with superior effort.*
   - *Genuinely proud of successes.*
   - *Shares the "good feeling" with others.*

The best part—the most satisfying component of W.E.—is the acknowledgment of the pride you feel when a job is completed and done well. It includes the knowledge that you did the work, did it well, and that you can enjoy credit for your success. You must engage your mind in order to take full advantage of the psychological effects of the feeling of pride. Pride is the payoff for your exemplary work ethic.

Assess engagement against "W.E." standards and expectations.

All the above criteria creates a template against which you will evaluate your engagement success at implementing the W.E. components. Follow these evaluation steps to ensure success.

1. Ensure clear W.E. expectations.
2. Watch for W.E. behaviors/attitudes.
3. Implement W.E. standards.

Each of these steps provide momentum for the evaluation phase of implementing W.E. (See sample evaluation form in the W.E. Tools section of this book.)

This evaluation process should be completed on a periodic basis to review how you are doing. On a regular basis an analysis must occur covering individual progress, achievements, challenges and milestones reached during a time frame. Tough as it is, you must also spend time discussing shortcomings and challenges. An evaluation of your progress will achieve the following goals.

- Review level of focus.
- Assess ability to stay on task.
- Evaluate success at being a team player.
- Measure ability to complete all aspects of a job.
- Determine quality and ability to exhibit pride.

Your measurement of individual success with a new or renewed work ethic will be more accurate when using W.E. standards that are consistent with expectations.

Careful what you Conceal.

I have always been a fairly outgoing person around others; however, from time to time I have run into individuals who have difficulty with this aspect of their lives. There was one girl who worked a brief assignment with me and my co-worker Carol. She (we'll call her Janet) would always shy away from groups of people and avoid direct contact with others she did not know. To my mind, she always seemed to be glancing over her shoulder as if watching for some unknown assailant. However, as a worker she was good. When Janet was given a specific, clearly communicated task, she was superior at focusing on the work and completing every aspect of the assignment. And she was quick, too. I have to say, I was impressed by the work ethic she displayed.

One day, while we had a brief break from our chores, the two of us were sitting in a private office. We were talking casually about the work when I decided to ask Janet about her family. I had hardly gotten the question out of my mouth, when she abruptly responded with . . . "I have no family." She went on to tell me the story of why she was by herself. It was because the CIA was after her. "I keep moving, since I know too much!" she said. "I have information that they want, so I carry a gun with me at all times in my purse just in case I get caught in a tight spot. That happened to me once you know." I was amazed and terrified at the sudden change in her tone and the admission that she was carrying a gun. Carrying a concealed weapon was strictly against our company policy. She quickly refocused her attention and then went back to work. Meanwhile, I slipped away to consult with security at our offices, and later informed Janet that her project work was complete. We thanked her for a fine job and sent her on her way.

"WE" Capsule: Make sure your W.E. efforts always stay grounded in the foundational beliefs of respect, fairness and ethical treatment for all individuals. It is key to your success!

CHAPTER 6

Ready, Set, Go!
How you'll implement your "W.E." initiative

Remember playing hide and seek when you were a child? If you were the seeker, you would stand in one place, cover your eyes and count to ten. At the end of your count you would announce . . . "Ready or not, here I come (go)!" Those words embody the spirit of taking on any important endeavor. Sometimes you just have to announce your intentions and go for it.

Every chapter in this book is designed to help you implement the W.E. process one step at a time. Your foundation is definitely an important step; however, if you take the initiative to do this process properly, your "ready, set, go!" step or implementation will become the most important factor in your ongoing success and your continued strength.

When implementing your W.E. initiative, it is essential to remember that the outcome of this process is to create a new foundation in work ethic values for you. Your values are essentially all of the things you stand for. Such was the case with my childhood. I was raised and learned in a safe environment where I understood early on the value of initiative and pitching in for the common good. Through focused and firm guidance, a strong foundation was laid for understanding the value of initiative. Since my parents helped establish this foundation, I took the next step by applying my work ethic in all that I did. My W.E. developed by knowing and doing what was right and necessary.

Through careful thought and planning I determined what my role and goals should be in life, and I carefully planned the process and defined the purpose of my goals.

Bon fires. My work ethic foundation wasn't just rules and directions, it included a lot of love, patience, values and guidance. My parents were wonderful role models. My fondest memories were of helping my Dad and Mom. One time in particular, I recall helping my Dad clear the fields of brush and debris for animal fences. I can remember being outside working under the clear blue Michigan sky on a gorgeous sunny fall day. I would pay attention to my Dad's directions, watch out for snakes, and work hard. We would stack the brush in large piles for removal or burning. He would always explain how and why we were doing a task. The family would spend many hours working together clearing a field and then later enjoy the evening around a brush fire telling stories and jokes, and laughing together. This closeness and shared time created a strong family bond.

Weed out the Weak, So the Strong Survive. I also learned to love growing things and about tending gardens. Each year my mother would have a large garden which stretched out for an acre or more. It was neatly laid out in sections and rows, and filled with a large variety of vegetables such as tomatoes, beans, peas, squash, cucumbers, sweet corn and much more. I recall that at one end we had a patch of strawberries along with some raspberry and blackberry bushes. I was amazed at how heartily the plants grew, in particular the weeds. I learned how the weeds would try to take over the garden and steal all the valuable water and nutrients in the soil from the plants. I made it my mission to keep the weeds out of our beautiful garden. I would spend hours weeding sections of the garden and tossing the remnants into a pile for drying or burning. It would make me smile with pride to survey a newly weeded section of the garden that was now free to grow and produce delicious foods.

I have to admit, I got much of my initiative and inspiration from watching my mom each season diligently clean and can or freeze our delicious harvest. Throughout the year we would enjoy her wonderfully prepared meals, vegetable dishes and homemade jellies and jams as a result. I even recall enjoying a mid-day snack right from the vine. There was nothing more tasty than a freshly salted tomato or cucumber, or a sweet, ripe strawberry. Even today, I think back with love and longing on those wonderful, purposeful days where I felt happy and at home.

Those stories express what I mean by initiative. A continual plan was implemented which ensured that we all enjoyed food, clothing and shelter. There are no short-cuts here. My parents provided a safe and caring learning environment, and I was the student. Care must always be taken to choose a path which is right for you based upon the foundation you have.

The following concepts will help you create the foundational components for your own W.E. initiative.

- Discovering what W.E. does.
- Deciding what to do.
- Setting the ground rules and standards.
- Highlighting best practices.

Discovering what "W.E." does.

First, we must start by outlining what work ethic can do for you. Your work ethic 1) defines your approach to work, 2) hones the skill of developing and implementing a plan, 3) increases your stamina to complete the work, and 4) expands your capacity to enjoy your accomplishments and achievements.

Have you begun to assess what your approach to work is?

Approaches to Work

- doer	or	- procrastinator
- leader	or	- follower
- pro-active	or	- reactive
- innovative	or	- methodical
- fast	or	- slow

W.E. has the capability to redefine what you stand for as well as establish your reputation in the community. What I mean is, your work ethic says a lot about you. It tells people that you care about your work as well as your reputation. Work ethic also displays to others that you have pride in your work and can be counted on to do what you say and to say what you'll do.

If you are running a business, W.E. can also change the way in which you look at hiring employees for your business. Here are some attributes to use when interviewing that will define your desired characteristics and aid in future recruitment of W.E.-centric individuals. Some basic W.E. attributes include:

Attribute	Question to determine Attribute
• ability to focus	How do you approach completing monotonous task?
• track record of work effort	When I say "accomplishments," what comes to mind?
• strong team orientation	Describe your method for working with others.
• ability to follow through	What is an effective way to ensure follow through?
• ability to multi-task	How do you handle/react to many priorities?
• innate pride in accomplishments	What gives you the biggest amount of pride?

You may develop other, slightly more specific attributes for your job candidates as you define and outline what W.E. means to you or your organization.

W.E. may also have performance outcomes that may not be easy to recognize at first. Some of these outcomes may include . . .

- • W.E. builds better work comprehension.
- • W.E. builds self esteem.

- W.E. offers opportunities for growth.
- W.E. changes lives.

Along the way you may also discover benefits and outcomes from W.E. that you may not have expected.

- Improved synergy between friends, acquaintances, teams, departments, etc.
- New workplace opportunities that support your W.E. initiative.
- Changes in your perception within the community due to your involvement.
- Increased communication between individuals, departments and other work units.

Decide Your "W.E." Plan

(Use this page to list your strengths, your support network and what you'll need)

Strengths—I can do the following . . .

1. _____
2. _____
3. _____
4. _____
5. _____

Support Network—who I can count on for moral support . . .

1. _____
2. _____
3. _____
4. _____
5. _____

Resources—what I will need to ensure success . . .

1. _____
2. _____
3. _____
4. _____
5. _____

Deciding what to do.

Everyone must decide to be engaged in order to have W.E. success. A key step to ensure full integration and engagement is the empowerment of individuals to become owners of their new culture of W.E. and their destiny. It is important to make sure you embrace the responsibility for your role in and the stake you have in the success of your new W.E. process.

On a larger scale, when bringing others on board, you may want to institute suggestion programs, feedback mechanisms, and a newsletter (or similar) dedicated to the implementation of W.E. Allow everyone access to ALL levels of leadership without lines of authority or chain of command. If you are truly committed to W.E., what purpose do the channels for communication serve but to stifle or discourage actual, resourceful and valuable feedback.

The essence of W.E. is "we" and that means allowing others to be a part of the plan. If you decide to develop committees or panels, be sure that representation from all levels of the organization are present on these teams to ensure engagement and aid understanding of how all decisions will affect everyone all the way to the front line. Additionally, all new actions or directions from these teams should be openly and regularly communicated to ensure transparency and accountability since everyone involved has a major stake in this initiative.

Even though you can tell people what to do, this method does not garner the best results. Communicating openly about your W.E. culture and asking for input, feedback and ideas from everyone, regardless of role, will help ensure you connect with those who will drive your success.

Setting the ground rules and standards.

A crucial step in laying your foundation for W.E. is establishing ground rules and standards. Consistency is the key element to effective rules and standards. Without ground rules individuals may proceed in the wrong direction and do more damage than good. Additionally, what you say you are going to do, you must do. Your credibility will be lost if you do not meet the expectations you've set with others and if you are not accountable to your rules and standards. Nothing kills motivation more quickly than hypocrisy.

Your ground rules should reflect your goals, ideals or the playing field for implementing a new vision. It is important to know what works, what people desire, and what motivates them. Your ground rules should also include expectations, time lines, feedback and accountability for results.

Here are my personal work ethic ground rules (minus any timeline).

"W.E." Ground rules

- We will make all **W**ork fun and interesting.
- We will **O**utline our W.E. plans with goals, dates and time lines.
- W.E. will **R**eward and appreciate our successes!
- We **K**eep our promises to one another while engaging our minds.
- **E**veryone holds the key to our success.
- We act as a **T**eam and support one another.
- Our final goal is to create new **H**abits and best practices.
- Commitment will be **I**ntegral to our success.
- W.E. will provide **C**ommunication to all on a regular basis.

Your standards might look something like those outlined above, or they may be tailored to meet the specific needs of your organization. All individuals must understand that they are partners in W.E. success and are going to be measured against the SAME standards for fairness and consistency. As appropriate, communication of your evaluation criteria regarding performance expectations, monetary rewards, other incentives, and the like, must be written to ensure consistency in content, intent, and application. Return to Chapter 5 for more criteria.

Highlighting best practices.

The last foundational step in building a W.E. culture is to establish and highlight the best practices that evolve out of your efforts. Best practices are those steps, processes and outcomes that most represent who you are and support your goals for a culture. They are proven successes which have occurred in your life, at your organization or in the community.

Best practices become most apparent over time. With W.E. it is ok to continue and bring with you your existing best practices.

However, you may find the new best practices will likely overtake your old practices over time.

Some examples of best practices might include items like the following:

- I can always be counted upon to do what I say I'll do.
- I am/we are active donors and volunteers in our community.
- I am/we are recognized as a top employer with diversity in the workforce.
- I/we participate in local schools and universities through scholarship programs.
- I/we can be relied upon to deliver our products/services on time, every time.
- I/we place the customer first and ensure follow through on my commitment.

Best practices are important because they provide a guideline for your actions, are representative of those characteristics you value, and establish standards and ethical foundations for the future.

When evaluating best practices, many of them may be determined to be a milestone as well. A milestone is a goal which was desired and ultimately achieved.

Here are a few examples of milestones achieved as a result of best practices.

- Increased my speed with completing daily chores, within 4 weeks, resulting in more family time.
- Reduced customer complaints by 50% due to increased customer service focus.
- Improved efficiency of order processing showing 30% quicker turnaround times in shipping and delivery times.
- Faster bank transaction processing (3 every 5 minutes) which means shorter waiting times at our bank teller windows.

It is important to have milestones in your life and plan, so that you are always challenged and strive to achieve more. The shear satisfaction of your accomplishments is one of the most rewarding outcomes of your W.E. efforts.

Remember, each step for implementing your work ethic foundation must be clearly understood and communicated to everyone including the hows and whys, allowances made for learning curves and thorough follow through and completion of every task.

You'll need to pay attention to details to ensure successful creation of your W.E. foundation.

CHAPTER 7

The Lincoln Logs® of "W.E."
Building a "W.E." culture

If you are a boomer, you may remember the original Lincoln Logs®. They were awesome, real wood, miniature toy logs with carved out notches at both ends of the log so that you could stack them at right angles to build a log house. They fit together so neatly that it resulted in a fairly strong toy house when you were done. Those logs acted as the support for the house and roof, and without them placed in proper order, the house would become wobbly and unstable, and then fall.

In order to build your own impactful W.E. house, you must be willing to put in place some key components that will support your life or business. Additionally, you must also be supportive to make changes in the way you see yourself as well as how you interact in our society. The following key ideas are provided to support your efforts. Each point is as important as the next when building your culture.

- Build (or rebuild) a culture, vision, mission.
- Get to know your friends, family, customers and business (again).
- Never forget where you came from.
- Choose to be a people person.

Build (or rebuild) your culture, vision and mission.

First, and foremost, start by building your W.E. culture; your way of thinking about W.E., with a solid vision and mission. Your culture defines who you are and what you stand for. It represents your beliefs and values, and is the "thread" which binds.

Incorporate the five W.E. components into all of your foundational beliefs: including values, standards, culture, vision, mission, branding, etc.

Everyone should have a vision and mission. Your vision is your plan for your future and how you'll get there, and your mission is what you want to achieve. Therefore, keep them current and make regular updates to the vision, mission and other aspects of your culture, in an effort to keep them from getting outdated or stale. Regularly adding or changing a few components in these statements is always a good idea.

Culture—defines who you are and what you stand for. It involves your heart-felt faith, values, beliefs, and ethics.

One company I worked for had an outstanding cultural foundation when I joined them. This company was all about working smart and valued relationships. Those aspects of the culture could be a solid cornerstone of any strong W.E. culture. When I was a part of the leadership team, we had great morale, a strong team and we supported one another well. As a team, we grew the company from a few sites to several around the nation in four or five years. The stock price rose quickly during that time. We achieved those records with hard work and dedication that was second to none. It was also because we had great synergy and a strong culture which tied us together. This culture emanated from the owners of the company and served to make us stronger and better. Unfortunately, it did not last. A new operations person came into power and decimated the culture, morale plummeted, and staff was driven away by poor philosophies and an unsuccessful leadership style. This person didn't understand or support the value of culture. Eventually the stock dropped down to record lows, into the single digits again. What happened? How did they lose their way? I believe that they failed to embrace those key aspects of the company culture, vision and mission which drove people to strive for more. They let financial decisions guide their way instead of the people and processes which created their success.

A strong culture defines who your are and what it is like to work in your company. It also determines what the experience will be like for your customers, primarily through superior service provided by satisfied employees. Therefore, everyone should incorporate aspects of work ethic which enliven and enrich your culture. To get you started, here are some phrases you might use:

- W.E. exhibit superior effort each and every day.
- W.E. is our promise; W.E. work hard because W.E. want to.
- Our work ethic shows in all that W.E. do.
- W.E. means you and me.
- W.E. strive for excellence in all that W.E. do.
- Our goal is to make sure W.E. meet our customers' needs.

CULTURE: **Beliefs** = your views, what you feel strongly about. **Ethics** = your honor, what you stand for. **Faith** = your convictions, does not have to have a religious component unless you want it to. **Heart** = your pulse, those passions that drive you to excel. **Values**—your principles, what you place in high priority.

Vision—your plan for the future and how you will get there.

Your vision should include your methods, how you will reach your desired goals. Make sure your vision for the future includes components of your Key to W.E. statement in your handbook, policies and employee orientation and all training. Also, add W.E. components into your performance evaluations and standards (See Chapter 4, for W.E. Standards). This will ensure that all employees are being evaluated and measured against the same expectations, and can help you achieve your plan.

Mission—what you strive for (goals) and what you hope to achieve.

Your mission is your goal: those things that you strive to do or be, what you want to achieve. Develop (or update) your mission to reflect your new W.E. culture. Display your W.E.-focused mission in public areas to announce to the world that you are W.E.-centric. A mission statement should include the following goals, methods, areas of emphasis, and intended outcomes.

- Goals—what you want to achieve.
- Methods—how you'll achieve them.
- Areas of emphasis—what you'll focus on doing, achieving.
- Intended outcomes—how you'll know you've met your goals.

Sample Mission:

"It is our goal to display a strong work ethic in all that we do. We will focus on our customers' needs, work together to meet those needs, act as a cohesive team, complete all work in a timely and thorough manner, and celebrate our accomplishments."

Once you have your culture, vision and mission defined, you can move forward with your W.E. plans.

Get to know your employees, customers, business partners and yourself (again).

When establishing your work ethic or a people-focused business model you may have to review all of your methods for dealing with others; friends, family, employees, customers, suppliers, target market, etc.

This means you should re-examine your policies for how you run your life or business. Here are some questions you should be asking yourself.

1. What is my purpose? My/our goal?
2. How will I conduct myself or my business going forward?
3. Is everything I do accomplished in an ethical manner?
4. What changes do I need to make to be in alignment?
5. What must I do to ensure consistency and follow-through?

It is important to reconnect with what you stand for and value, as well as how you interact with these individuals that impact your life or business. Make sure you have built or can establish strong relationships that are based upon respect, ethics and mutual interests.

This process of reconnecting may feel like a sole searching effort, and to some extent it is just that. However, in order to "reconnect" effectively, you must be willing to objectively assess who you are and what you stand for. Here are a few ways to assess your psyche, intentions, and motivations. Ask yourself these types of questions:

- Do I place value on my reputation?
- Are those that I know and deal with of good character?
- Am I honest and sincere about what I want in life or expect from people?

After reflecting upon these types of questions, complete the survey on the next page.

How Well do I Know ME (my ethics)?

One of life's biggest challenges is to truly know ourselves. When we learn to become comfortable with who we are—our appearance, behaviors, actions and decisions, are at their best! Then we are free to achieve all our life's dreams. When you know yourself, you will exude confidence. With confidence you can achieve anything. Rate how well you know you!

SELF ESTEEM. Answer these Questions by Circling the Best response:
(There may be multiple right answers, and a little humor, but only one answer truly represents you.)

	Scoring Points

1. *Do you have pride in your appearance?*

a. Only on "good" days.   b. Yes, I am happy with me!
c. I haven't looked in the mirror lately.   ____

2. *Do you believe others deserve dignity and respect at all times?*

a. Heck no!   b. Respect. People have to earn it!
c. Yes, because I want to receive it too!   ____

3. *Do you place value on your ethics and reputation?*

a. No, I do not care.   b. It depends on who's asking.
c. Yes, they matter to me!   ____

4. *Are you approachable and welcome individuals to come talk to you?*

a. No, but I'd try.   b. Yes, I enjoy talking to new people.
c. Heck no! Leave me alone.   ____

5. *Do you dwell on your mistakes and sometimes consider yourself a failure?*

a. Sure. Reality sucks!   b. I suppose. If it's a dumb
mistake.   c. No, I learn and move on.   ____

Subtotal

____

CONSIDERATION for OTHERS. Checkmark Yes or No for Each:

These questions relate to your respect/ consideration for others.	YES	NO	
Do you treat others with dignity and respect at all times?	____	____	____
Do you give time or resources ($$) for good causes or charity?	____	____	____
Do you believe that most people are good at heart and honest?	____	____	____
When people are rude to you or others, are you rude back to them?	____	____	____
If you saw someone who was in trouble, would you stop to help?	____	____	____

Subtotal

____

DECISION MAKING. Checkmark Yes or No for Each: **YES**   **NO** | Scoring Points

Are you able to access all information for a sound, quick decision?   ____   ____ | ____

Do you consider all outcomes/consequences when making decisions?   ____   ____ | ____

When making a tough decision, can you feel confident about it?   ____   ____ | ____

Do you consider the input of others useful when facing a decision?   ____   ____ | ____

Do you place a high priority on having all the facts before deciding?   ____   ____ | ____

Subtotal

____

Answers:
See Scoring Guide (back of book) for assessing how well you know you.

Total =

____

SCORING: I Know "ME" = 85-100 pts., Getting to Know "ME" = 70-84 pts., Unsure About "ME" = 55-69 pts, Don't Know "ME" = 54 or less points

---

Never forget where you came from.

A very important concept when developing your W.E. is to ensure that you never forget your roots and that you learn from the mistakes of the past. Our life lessons are important to us because they become the starting point from which we can grow and change. When you think about it, our behaviors are what define us, and learning from our mistakes should provide us with the catalyst for change. Once you recognize that you need to make improvements, or don't like how you've behaved or what you used to stand for, you can then pull yourself up and declare that "it is time for change!"

This humbling, soul-searching experience may feel like an awkward one, however it is a valuable one as well. Everyone knows an example or two of individuals and companies that have been at the brink of ruin and turned things around.

Here are some examples:

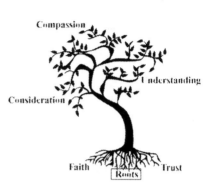

- Lee Iacocca and Chrysler
- Brittany Spears
- Donald Trump

I have experienced individuals in the course of my life who have behaved deplorably. In many cases those are individuals who have risen to positions of authority and then become "drunk with power." They act as though they are "God's gift" to the world and that those around them are fools. I have watched those situations time and again, and asked myself . . . "When did they lose their way? How did they become so corrupted?" Well, in my opinion, they forgot their roots, where they came from, and the value of treating others with respect.

If you ever risk becoming too "full of yourself" or forgetting your roots, you need to reconnect to where you came from by listing who you are and what you are thankful for, as follows. Insert a couple of your own realizations.

What I Stand for . . .	What I Am Thankful for . . .
• work ethic	• my compassion for others
• honesty and integrity	• never compromising my ethics
_____	_____
_____	_____
_____	_____
_____	_____

Our "roots" create the foundation of our beliefs and connect us to the truly meaningful aspects of our lives such as compassion, understanding and consideration. When we can stay grounded we learn that there are behaviors we **DO NOT WANT** to ever have as a part of our life or our being.

Choose to be a people person.

The most effective W.E. personality is an outgoing and genuine personality. If you do not possess either of these characteristics, you will need to become comfortable with them. Being a people person, an outgoing and approachable person, and having the ability to ask questions, initiate conversations and hold discussions will allow you to experience a side of other people which is enlightening and rewarding. If you are an approachable person, people will come to you with ideas and concerns, and this will allow you to take the "temperature" of your relationships or work place. In that way you can help others. First, ask yourself, do I have the following characteristics?

Approachable people.	Outgoing people.
• Welcoming	• Friendly
• Receptive	• Positive
• Sincere	• Comfortable (with themselves)
• Genuine	• Talkative

People-focused persons will achieve more with and through others. They have the ability to instill confidence in others through their believable and positive nature. I once had a boss, Joe, who taught me many of life's valuable lessons, however I didn't know it at the time. I was busy going through some personal turmoil (a separation, divorce) when I knew Joe, and he was there for me like a rock—patient and understanding. He would listen to my worries and fears and provide the occasional word of advice, and then focus my energies toward a resolution. He had the ability to show compassion and understanding, and then re-direct my focus on the positive. One day, when I was having a bad day, not knowing what my future plan should be he helped me get on track by focusing my attention on how I could attain a better future. He suggested that I go to college and get an education so that I could build skills for my future. He challenged me to work on new projects and assignments, designed to test my abilities, so I could learn. He was a role model and friend whom I will never forget.

"WE" Capsule: Make sure your W.E. efforts always stay grounded in the foundational beliefs of respect, fairness and ethical treatment for all individuals. It is key to your success!

SECTION 3

Maintaining "W.E."

CHAPTER 8

Cheerleading "W.E."
Keeping the spirit of "W.E." alive

When I was in high school I used to be in the band. I played clarinet and had to memorize many marching routines and spirited tunes designed to inspire the crowds at our football games each fall. Our role was to motivate the fans with sound and motion that served to rouse their spirit for the team and a winning game.

Just as with any important thing that you do in your life, you must be a cheerleader at times to ensure the spirit of your efforts is kept alive and well. One of the more important steps in the process of implementing a W.E. culture, vision, mission and plan is to ensure that the spirit of your good intentions are kept alive.

We are all born with the potential for a solid work ethic. Unfortunately it only takes root effectively in a select few people. Typically, once you understand what work ethic can do for you and when you experience the rewards, benefits and outcomes of your W.E. efforts, you are hooked. W.E. is not a fad or a flavor of the month. Clearly, W.E. is everyone's responsibility. To bring everyone on board, at home or at work, you will need a coordinated effort to help ensure engagement, spirit and an effective and ongoing implementation.

All too often, individuals with the power or influence to effect change pass the buck to those who have no ability to ensure success of the effort. Don't make that mistake. If those who are instrumental in the inception of W.E. do not step up and guide the process or support the tenants of their own ideas—they will fail. Here are a few tips for avoiding failure and keeping your spirit of W.E. alive.

- Incorporate W.E. into all that you do.
- Show W.E. leadership early on.
- Outline W.E. expectations for all.
- Reward and recognize every W.E. effort.

Be creative in your endeavors. Empower all individuals to identify ways to keep the spirit alive. Don't let the spirit of W.E. die because an effort is not made or the focus is not there.

Incorporate "W.E." into all that you do.

Establishing a W.E. culture involves more than just a few words on a piece of paper. The last thing you want is for W.E. to be something no one cares about. You need to ensure all aspects of your life or business are saturated with W.E. components.

- Set W.E. goals	- Establish W.E. standards
- Outline W.E. steps	- Develop a W.E. vision/mission
- Include W.E. in all correspondence	- Put W.E. language into all documents.

Show W.E. leadership early on.

A key to your success is to walk, talk, eat and breathe W.E. Effective leadership is the key to this effort. You and every member of your team must be engaged and accountable for his/her attitude and actions. Everyone must be outgoing, effective at communication, aware of the goals, and accountable for results. Your progress must be measured and individuals rewarded for his/her success with implementing W.E.

Here are some suggestions for effective and accountable W.E. leadership.

- Share your plan and strategy with leaders first.
- Set clear W.E. expectations.

- Make sure every person understands his/her role
- Define their part in the new W.E. process.
- Hold your people accountable for success and meeting deadlines.

At your organization, for example, measure the success of your staff, supervisors and leaders in the following manner. Their success may be best measured through employee surveys, focus groups and other feedback tools. Whatever process you choose to obtain this feedback, look for these signs:

- Quality of customer service in their areas of responsibility (internal or external).
- Positive feedback on effectiveness of the staff (perception of customers).
- Effectiveness and frequency of communication (types and creative distribution).
- Fairness and consistency of treatment of all people (equal opportunity for all).
- Levels of turnover and attrition in their areas of responsibility (trending up/down).

You may come up with additional measurement tools as appropriate for your situation; however, make sure you pay attention to levels of engagement. If even one person is not on board, it could spell trouble. One "bad apple" can do a lot of damage with a negative attitude or lack of effort.

Outline clear expectations for all.

To get everyone engaged and accountable for the same results, you must outline clear expectations. These expectations should include the following types of actions:

- Support for the power of W.E.
- Exhibit W.E. spirit every day.

- Act in an ethical manner at all times.
- Perform to the best of your ability.
- Support your team or department.
- Provide your feedback when requested.

Don't expect everyone to be up to speed with these expectations immediately. Some individuals are more receptive and quick to catch on, while others may be more hesitant and less outgoing. Take time to indoctrinate everyone carefully and thoroughly.

Reward and Recognize (R&R) W.E. spirit!

Get creative here! Instead of rolling out the types of functions or actions you think will motivate and reward people, let your people tell you what they value. Hold creative contests which solicit feedback from people on what rewards they value and what functions they would like to participate in. Remember to include other incentives for the best ideas too. Do this regularly so that your R&R functions and ideas don't get stale or dull.

Below are some R&R ideas for encouraging feedback and rewarding input from staff . . .

- Get a day off with pay (R&R) for having the best new idea.
- Earn a $100 gas card for sharing your perspective (on surveys).
- Win free attendance at an upcoming seminar (outside the company).

The best places to work ensure the work is fun and the environment a pleasant one. Here are some other ideas to motivate and support W.E.

1. Develop your support network—W.E. Diplomats
2. Hire people who possess your W.E. attributes. (See Chapter 6)
3. Make sure all your communication has W.E. spirit!

Your goal is to keep individuals always thinking about how to make W.E. more successful in their lives, workplace or the organization. They are less likely to blame others for shortcomings or lack of creativity if they are brought into the process directly.

"WE" Capsule: Make sure your W.E. efforts always stay grounded in the foundational beliefs of respect, fairness and ethical treatment for all individuals. It is key to your success!

Best application in a business environment.	**Key to Your Success** **"W.E." Diplomats**

A Diplomat program is a great way to get your W.E. efforts off the ground while building and maintaining morale during your implementation and beyond. It will be important to select individuals in your organization who have a confident personality, are good communicators and have the desire to be engaged in this process. These Diplomats will drive the spirit, keep communication lines open, and ensure an effective implementation by keeping in touch with all individuals within your organization.

Defined: A role model and cheerleader who embodies all the characteristics of your W.E.: focus, follow through, spirit, team player, etc. and is respected by their peers.

Criteria: To select the best individuals to help lead your campaign to build a culture and new way of thinking each candidate must meet the following criteria . . .

- Individuals who are in good standing. (no performance issues)
- No higher role with the organization than supervisor. (no management staff.*)
- Individuals with a solid work ethic and record of top performance. (achiever)
- People who focus their efforts on taking care of the customer. (internal/external)
- Individuals who enjoy all aspects of their job and career. (good attitude)
- No current disciplinary action in their personnel file within one year.

---

* Management has the effect of intimidating employees and gaining participation out of fear.

Role and Responsibilities: The individuals who act as W.E. Diplomats will be responsible for the following tasks, role and responsibilities:

- Act as cheerleader for your W.E. (work ethic) initiative.
- Operate as the eyes and ears of the organization—watch for W.E. behaviors, reward W.E. efforts, and listen well to all feedback from staff.
- Participate in all W.E.-centric functions and efforts.
- Communicate effectively and proactively with staff and leadership.
- Maintain a professional appearance, fresh outlook and positive W.E. attitude.
- Continue to perform their job at a superior level, displaying W.E. always.

Develop an application process for interested parties. Have a committee of both employees and management interview and select your new W.E. Diplomats.

CHAPTER 9

Riding the "W.E." roller Coaster.
Work Ethic of the future

Establishing work ethic may feel like a roller coaster ride at times—with the ups and downs you may face. However, the positive outcomes you can expect for your future surely outweigh any challenges you might face along the way. Building W.E. includes the exhilaration of a fantastic ride to a great, new, focused future.

It is my intent that through focused efforts described in this book we can bring back the tried and true work ethic practices of the past to build a stronger work—focused society for a new and improved future.

Here are a few ways in which I believe you can accomplish a smooth W.E. process.

- Buckle yourself in. Place emphasis on contributions and efforts.
- Focus is on individuals. *(Ok, everyone's hands in the air!)*
- Experience the ups and downs. Learn lessons from the past.
- Never forget where you came from.
- Establish best practices for the future.
- Build a new work culture. *(Come on. Let's go ride again!)*

All of these things can be accomplished as long as you don't view W.E. as a one time effort. W.E. has to be a new way of life. It is a personal effort which brings about a great, new future.

Buckle yourself in. Place emphasis on contributions.

Just like on a roller coaster, you need to buckle yourself in for the ride. You need to prepare yourself mentally for the short term with W.E. including the turns, dips, loops and drops to come.

For You. As you implement your plan to build your new W.E., you must focus your thoughts on contributions. Contributions are the efforts or steps you make toward attaining a stronger work ethic. Here are some examples of how you can emphasize change.

- I choose to see the good in me, other people, the world.
- I conscientiously changed "my behavior" today.
- I finally completed a project that I'd been putting off.

Remember, no one can change their behaviors over night—it is a step by step process. Every contribution you make is a step in the right direction toward a brighter future.

At Your Organization. When your W.E. efforts are in full swing, it will be important to focus communication and appreciation efforts on recognizing those ongoing contributions and accomplishments that have been made. A sure fire method for success is to highlight the efforts of those people who will ensure your success. Below are some examples which should be charted so they will be noticed, measured and rewarded.

Name	Contribution	Organization	reward
Dave	Increase in sales leads. Improved customer service.	XYZ Manuf.	Day off
Karen	Reduced customer wait time at teller lines.	Peoples Bank	$100.00
Cathy	Reductions in customer complaints on returns.	Joelle's Store	Seminar

Some other examples of efforts include, reduced lines at checkout lanes, faster call pick-up at the reception desk, and decreases in customer service complaints—all which will become apparent and should be charted for all to see.

As noted in Chapter 8, don't be afraid to solicit new ideas and areas of focus from your staff. Remember, if you seek new ways to extract W.E. ideas from your people, you must also have creative and different ways to recognize and reward those contributions.

Focus is on individuals.

With W.E. it is essential that the focus be paid specifically on individual efforts. As I have said, this needs to be an effort which will change the way you operate your life or business forever, so everyone in your life needs to be involved and engaged. Do not make this "just another attempt" at change. Everyone, especially you, must be held accountable for change.

However, there is one caveat, always remember that we are talking about people here. No two personalities are the same. Some people are shy, some are loud. Some people are focused, some are creative. Some are easy going, some are high strung. Whatever their outlook on life, albeit, the world, it has value—it has merit, even if the only lesson is to learn how you don't want to act or behave. Remember, make sure your W.E. efforts always stay grounded in the foundational beliefs of respect, fairness and ethical treatment for all individuals. That is your key to success!

Learn lessons from the past.

It is always important to remember that we can learn from our mistakes. You may have had some embarrassing moments or made a bad decision in the past, and at the same time another person may just be learning the ropes. However, when we share our experiences and talk about our lessons, we keep others from making the same mistakes we did.

Ask yourself these kinds of questions.

- What has worked in the past?
- What did we do that didn't work so well?
- What were our biggest successes?
- Where did we make mistakes?
- What can we learn from those mistakes?
- How can we avoid those same mistakes in the future?

Lessons are those things we do to Learn (in) Each Situation (that) Some Obstacles Nurture Success. If we can learn from the lessons of the past, we may not be doomed to repeat them.

L	-	Learn
E	-	Each
S	-	Situation
S	-	Some
O	-	Obstacles
N	-	Nurture
S	-	Success

Finally, it is essential that we stay grounded as we learn from those lessons and mistakes of the past so we can move beyond them into a better future.

Never forget where you came from.

One of the toughest lessons in life, for each of us, is to learn to keep our life and our success in perspective. We have to remember not to let position, status or money corrupt or influence who we are or how we treat others. This is easier said than done, primarily because it is human nature to gain an ego when we have status, power or money.

However, if you work at it, it can be done. Through conscious effort and faith, you can remember your roots and make it a priority to show respect for the treatment of others. When you are able to accomplish this task, you will be a better person for it. When you think about it, we are no more or no less than what we stand for. And if what you stand for is good and ethical, you'll know it in your heart and soul. You do not want to spend a lifetime wrestling with your conscience. In the end, what we all truly want, is to be accepted for who and what we are.

Establishing best practices for the future.

A key outcome from establishing a W.E. culture or lifestyle are that those new behaviors may be identified as best practices in your future. As mentioned in Chapter 6, this final step in implementing a W.E. culture is intended to help you establish best practices that evolve out of your efforts. Yes, best practices can take time to develop, however by putting yourself into the mindset of watching for improvements that are made over time, you will better achieve the change. One step which will evaluate how you are doing building best practices, is to qualify and quantify those practices you deem noteworthy. You will want to ask yourself these types questions.

1. How will these best practices represent who you are?
2. Which best practices will help you establish a solid W.E. framework?
3. Do these best practices support your culture, vision and mission?
4. Are you recognized for your best practices within your circle of friends?

Best practices are essential because they establish a framework for your future actions, are representative of those characteristics you value, and result in established standards and ethical foundations for your W.E. culture.

Best practices are those actions, processes and outcomes that most represent who you have become, support your goals for a

W.E. culture, and are proven successes in your life, company and/or community.

Build a Work Culture.

Your building blocks for a W.E. culture should look something like the next diagram. You start with a foundation, just as with any building, the strength of which holds it up. Then you move into a learning process where you share ideas, create new focus and instruct one another along the way. Once understanding has been accomplished, you observe, share and benefit from the focus and engagement of others. As you do so, you gain momentum toward success. Next you must reward and recognize those efforts made toward a W.E. environment in creative ways to keep the spirit of W.E. alive.

The final step is the identification of best practices which have resulted from all of your efforts. We are talking about those steps you took or ideas you implemented which resulted in effective efforts to establish W.E. and thereby may be best practices. When you find you have developed some best practices you are on your way to W.E. success.

Remember, you will always have the ability to add, change or remove steps along the way. However, these building blocks will definitely provide structure and guide you as you implement your W.E. cultural change.

"WE" Capsule: Make sure your W.E. efforts always stay grounded in the foundational beliefs of respect, fairness and ethical treatment for all individuals. It is key to your success!

CHAPTER 10

A "W.E." Glee Club.
What "W.E." success will look like

There is nothing more important than keeping the spirit of your work ethic effort alive, and doing so may appear more like a Glee Club than a W.E. club. However, a very important part of the W.E. process will be to make sure you keep your sense of humor alive and well and that you do not take yourself too seriously. That is why I call this chapter the W.E. Glee Club.

This last, but definitely not least, important step in the process of implementing a W.E. culture is so important that you could fail without it. It is essential that you remember to assess and admire the successes you've achieved. It is important to appreciate what success looks like with a W.E. culture. Here are some "Glee—focused" concepts that'll help you evaluate the success of your new W.E. efforts.

- Value making a contribution.
- W.E.s double meaning.
- Take pride (glee) in a job well done.
- Return of customer service.
- What makes W.E. so impactful.
- What will be your contribution?

What will success look like when you implement W.E. in your life or your organization? It will be a reflection of the effort you have put into it. It will feel like learning made easier because that's essentially what you've done. You've taken the basic human need for learning and focused it on one important goal. Work ethic may well turn out to be the most important change you will ever make.

Value making a contribution.

When you have engaged your W.E. you will not only have increased motivation, but your outlook on life will improve because you'll have a goal. When people have a goal they are focused on improving their future. Engaged individuals tend to be more satisfied, productive and focused. Your W.E. process may manifest itself in ways you didn't expect. You'll find more satisfaction helping other people. It comes easier when you feel good about yourself. You will notice improvements in customer service both internal and external. When you have a strong work ethic you feel pride in making a contribution to the welfare of others and ultimately to your future.

The Power of Work Ethic

"One of the lasting lessons I learned as I was growing up was to be proud of a good day's work. There is pride in accomplishing a task and making a contribution, especially one that helps out your family. For each contribution you become a stronger person. When your contribution produces good outcomes, you will feel the power of work ethic."

A solid work ethic is the key to your success. You may not realize it, but you have the power over your future and can build your self esteem along the way if you take control of your life, become a contributor, and are accountable for your future.

"W.E."s double meaning.

I have established W.E. to mean work ethic in this book, but ironically it also has it's standard connotation of "us, all of us, together." Of course, this is perfect for my purposes. Any new culture or effort cannot stand on words alone, it has to be backed up with good intentions. W.E. will be its most successful if everyone in your life is on board and supporting the goal. Here is an illustration of the double meaning.

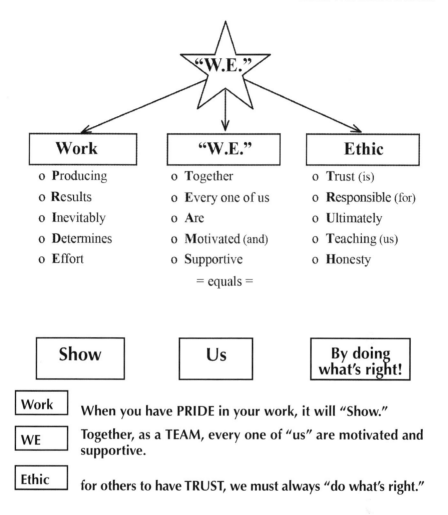

Take pride (glee) in a job well done.

The return of pride in a job well done is one of the most rewarding outcomes of W.E. When individuals experience the self esteem and joy of making a valued contribution or achieving their dreams, they become filled with pride.

There are a number of creative ways to express pride in W.E. especially if you encourage ideas from others. Invent your own or solicit "slogans" from others to emphasize W.E. goals. If used in a pro-active manner your new slogans can build morale, aid in communication, and instill pride. You may need to come up with your own or hold contests and competitions to find new ideas for W.E. slogans. Here are a few examples:

- W.E. take pride in a job well done.
- W.E. is better than ME.
- W.E. can take care of YOU!

It is fun and motivational for individuals to be included in the process of developing slogans, etc. and earning prizes or other benefits for their ideas. It's even more fun to see new ideas used in your W.E. efforts provide inspiration and motivation for its success.

Return of customer service.

When you feel part of something bigger than yourself, part of a larger goal, then you tend to pay more attention to your work and make a better effort with your daily work product. With properly implemented W.E. efforts—including clear Standards and Expectations—you will experience an improvement in relationships and ultimately in customer service.

"W.E." Expressions

Here are some wonderful expressions that communicate W.E. intentions. Some of them are familiar to me from my childhood and others are new. Feel free to use them.

- Many hands make light work.
- Good things come to those who work hard for them.
- If we all pitch in, the work will go faster.
- It's important to finish the job completely.
- A hard day's work is the greatest satisfaction.
- Everyone here carries their own weight.
- Everything in life is better when you earn it.

You can inspire others to greater achievement if you are a good role model and sincere in your satisfaction with their progress.

> **"WE" Capsule:** Make sure your W.E. efforts always stay grounded in the foundational beliefs of respect, fairness and ethical treatment for all individuals. It is key to your success!

What makes "W.E." so impactful, so important?

Implementing an effective W.E. lifestyle requires a receptive mind, willingness to see beyond, and the ability to commit to change. There exists a wide spectrum of concepts which influence success. Here are a few of those influences:

- **Drive**

W.E. is all about drive. Drive for success. Drive to be better than before. Drive to do things in a better, more complete way.

- **Accomplishment/achievement**

W.E. is all about accomplishments and achievements. It's about reaching for the stars and not stopping until you get there. It's about celebrating your successes.

- **Belonging**

W.E. is belonging. It's being part of a team, an effort, and something more than just YOU. W.E. is working together to achieve a common goal. It's about pride in being a part of something bigger than you.

- **Personal and Business success**

W.E. is success! It is about putting skills to work to make personal strides, individual performance better, customer service better, and even the organization better. It's about improving your bottom line because everyone is on board with what the goal is, what is expected of them, and where you are heading. It's about being better than your competition! It's profitability!

- **Pride**

W.E. is all about pride. Pride in who you are—who you've become. Pride in who you'll be. W.E. is about letting that inner pride show. It's about being happy about what you have done and where you are going.

- **Honor**

W.E. is your badge of honor. It is about doing the right thing and knowing it. It is about integrity and effort. It is about keeping your promises and following through. It involves not letting yourself, your family or your team down.

- **Commitment**

W.E. is commitment. It is commitment to yourself to focus your efforts. It is being there for your team (family). It is about going above and beyond, and being successful at it. When we share our commitment, we have a bond that will last a lifetime.

What will be your Contribution?

We all have a desire to make a contribution. For some, it is a driving force in our lives. Some individuals want to make their mark on society, fulfill a dream, or be remembered for some major accomplishment. If that describes you, then you must make a plan to focus your efforts on that goal. After all, in many ways it is our goals and achievements which make us feel alive, engaged and more connected to our world.

The biggest reward you can have in life is to look back at what you've done, how you've contributed, and enjoy the pride of achievement. It is my belief that our very soul needs this kind of nourishment. Without contribution, we sometimes feel unfulfilled, and may even suffer remorse at not having left a legacy or made any contribution whatsoever.

Whatever your dream, work ethic is a choice. It is up to you to choose your own path. It may surprise you to discover that you never really know what you are capable of until you try. A solid work ethic can bring you all the best things in life if you allow it. So, get out there and fulfill your life's dream. Good luck!

CHAPTER 11

"W.E." Pay Day.
The Benefits of "W.E."

WE, WE, WE . . . all the way to the bank!

W.E. is success! It is about putting skills to work to make personal strides, individual performance better, customer service better, and even the organization better. It's about improving your bottom line because everyone is on board with what the goal is, what is expected of them, and where you are heading. It's about being better than your competition! It's profitability!

Bringing work ethic into your future can have multiple positive results and permeate all aspects of your life. Below I have outlined the benefits that I have experienced from my work ethic and those that you can expect as well if you give your all.

1. Staying fit with "W.E."

Because I have a strong work ethic, I stay active and thereby fit. There is not a day that goes by where I have not completed a project from my long list of "I'll get to that" type of projects. How do I do that, you may ask?

- I focus on what I want to accomplish. Place the task on my list.
- I determine a time that suits my schedule as well as the project.
- I complete the project, in its entirety, at that time.
- I sit back and feel good about the achievement.

I have focused my mind and therefore can get to and complete the projects that I deem important. The outcome of completing these projects is progress and success.

- My mind is clear from focus on that task.
- My body is active and thereby more fit.
- My stamina is good and normal for my age.
- My overall health is good and normal for my age.

Staying fit includes clearing your mind of clutter and baggage. I stay fit mentally as well because I do not dwell on the negative or perceive things as impossible or unachievable. Along the way, I also get physical exercise since many of my projects require some level of physical effort.

2.   Staying focused with "W.E."

My W.E. keeps me focused on the future of my business and the needs of my family. I am constantly thinking . . . "What can I accomplish today?" With focus in mind, how can W.E. help you like it has helped me?
- Keep things in perspective.
- Create sound mental practices. Place issues on list—cross things off list.
- Focus on the positive "can do's" not on the negative.

3.   Finding my self esteem.

My childhood introduction to work ethic resultantly permeated all aspects of my life but none more significantly than my self esteem. I have a strength of character and confidence as a result of my belief in the importance and value of W.E.

- I am not afraid to try new things.
- I pick up new concepts easily.

- I do not shy away from challenges.

My new-found self esteem has provided me with the following characteristics.

- A "stick to it" attitude.
- Confidence.
- Receptive to people/ideas.
- Strength of character.
- Willingness to learn.

Anyone can build these characteristics to ensure a successful and satisfactory life.

4.　Drive to succeed.

I have found that my W.E. has helped me so many times in my life just by providing the necessary drive for success. Every time that I have had doubt about what to do in a situation; like a major life change (divorce/job loss), or helping out in my community (philanthropy), my W.E. drive has kicked in and helped me find strength and courage.

5.　Willingness to learn and try new things.

My receptive mind has allowed me to open up to new possibilities and to consider new concepts/ideas/ways of doing things. My willingness to learn has provided many wonderful experiences which have enhanced my abilities and opened up new opportunities for me. Here are a few characteristics that may benefit you:

- Open minded.
- Receptive to new ideas.

- Creativity and originality
- Always learning and growing.

This W.E. benefit of willingness may be the most significant because I believe the only thing that holds each of us back from success is our own self-imposed limitations.

CLOSING

Before I close, I want to say a little more about the importance of the customer service experience. In my opinion, enhancement of the customer experience is the most critical issue that we face. This experience influences the success of any business and speaks to the importance placed on respect in our society.

Why then is there far too little attention paid to the people who create these customer experiences? For example, how many of us remember where we bought an item we recently purchased when questioned about it? Not too many. However, when asked about our customer experience, how we were treated, how quickly we can clearly recall how we were treated and exactly what happened at the time, especially if it was a bad experience. Interesting, isn't it, that we can immediately recall the details of a negative scenario as opposed to a positive one. The outcome from all this disconnect is the disillusioned customer who has lost faith in businesses' ability to embrace their needs.

If respect is not being taught at home, how can it magically manifest in people? How many people don't understand or have never learned to value this basic human need? Far too often we watch and allow disrespectful treatment of others—without consequence. If we allow the ignorant to act without respect, they denigrate the customer experience and our society. We should be teaching respect and empowerment, and providing positive role modeling as well as constructive feedback to change bad behaviors.

Why not put W.E. to work and build understanding, work ethic and strong foundations, all at the same time. Work ethic can provide those things and bring back the importance of respectful treatment. Regardless of how your life has played out up to this point, the contents of this book will provide you with a plan for making changes in your future. W.E. is an essential tool which will aid in making your dreams of personal and financial success come true. You only have to believe to make it happen. It all comes down to W.E.

"W.E." TOOLS
FOR INDIVIDUALIZED PLANS AND
"W.E." ASSESSMENT SCORING
GUIDES EVERYDAY "W.E."

One concept that has helped me to be successful with my work ethic is my "everyday" plan. These days, these thoughts and these ideas are every bit a part of my fiber and being. I often plan out the day in my thoughts the night before, knowing full well what I want and need to accomplish.

I have to say, it has worked for me. I tend to accomplish more because of the structure of my thoughts and henceforth my day. Here is an outline of that plan:

"W.E." Action Plan:

1. You start each day knowing what you want and need to accomplish.
2. You make a plan. Plan out your day.
3. You visualize what your day will look like, even down to the route you'll take and the time you'll require.
4. You make sure you have all your paperwork, coupons and packages.
5. You understand the value of accomplishments.
6. You don't put more on your plate that you can handle.

Example of a "W.E." Day:

Chore Order	Task	Where it is	Time Allot.	Direction
1.Leave home	chores	travel to bank	2 minutes	outbound
2.Bank	deposit	1 mile from home	10 minutes	outbound
3.Post office	mail	5 miles from home	10 minutes	outbound
4.Grocery store*	shopping	2 miles from home	30 minutes	inbound
5.Pharmacy	prescription	1 mile from home	5 minutes	inbound
6.Home	complete	travel home	3 minutes	inbound

* any planned trip to the grocery store must take into consideration food spoilage and thereby chore order.

Sample "W.E." Day

I felt it might be valuable to provide a sample of what a day looks like for me when I map out a plan for getting my work done that day. It isn't just random thought and chance coordination. I clearly evaluate and outline what would be the best way to "attack" my day and accomplish what I need and want to get done.

Here is a basic outline of what happens and what goes on in my head as I plan my day.

1. Get up to pre-set alarm.
2. Give yourself 15-30 minutes to wake up, ease into the day.
3. Mentally visualize your day; what you need to accomplish.
4. Consider all factors: all responsibilities, deadlines, family, friends.
5. Gather all necessary paperwork, coupons and packages, etc.
6. Map out a plan in your head or on paper (or both)
7. Make best use of time; multi-task.
8. Include down time to re-coup from a busy schedule.

I am a realistic person, however, many times I try to cram too much work into too little time. When that happens, unless there is a deadline, I don't fret about it and move the project to the next day. It is best if you don't stress about things which are out of your control or incomplete projects.

I am, however, here to give you a few pointers on how to make the most of your time.

1. Keep things organized. Know where your "work to be done" is located.
2. Make a list of what you want to accomplish. Stick to your list.
3. Don't let distractions deter you.
4. Projects that aren't completed one day fall over onto the next day's list.
5. Take pride, feel good about what you got done. Keeps you motivated for tomorrow.

Plan Your Day

Chore	Priority (in order)

"Work Ethic" Assessment Scoring Guide

Determining your "W.E." score.

To determine your W.E. score, use the following point value guide by applying the points based upon your responses. Record your score on the Assessment Tool page in the column provided on the right side and total that column to obtain your overall score.

Give yourself the corresponding points based upon answering Yes or No.

Question:	YES	NO
Are you pleasant to be around in the morning? Do you smile?	5	2
Do you make a list on paper/in your head of what you'll do today?	5	0
Do you make your bed each morning/day?	5	2
Do you conscientiously think about how your work affects others?	5	0
Do you begin your day by putting things in order at home/work?	5	1
Can you work as part of a team/group without having center stage?	5	0
Do you believe in the value of learning something new every day?	5	1
Can you finish a job all alone even when others should be helping?	5	0
Do you clean up your office/home before you finish for the day?	5	2
Do you have pride and a sense of accomplishment from your work?	5	0

Give yourself those points which correspond with the answer you circled.

1. What are your first thoughts at the start of your day?

a. I gotta pee! b. Whose life can I destroy today? c. What will I accomplish today?

| a. = 5 points | b. = 0 points | c. = 10 points |

2. When you encounter a challenge in your work, day, or life, what do you think?

a. This sucks, I quit! b. I'll wait till someone tells me what to do. c. I bet I can figure this out!

| a. = 0 points | b. = 3 points | c. = 10 points |

3. When everyone else takes off and leaves you doing the work, how do you respond?

a. This sucks, I quit! b. I can get this work done for now. c. Everyone sure is lazy. I quit!

| a. = 0 points | b. = 10 points | c. = 3 points |

4. If you are struggling with completing a project, what is your first thought?

a. I'll get help. b. Who can I throw under the bus? c. No one is helping me!?

| a. = 10 points | b. = 0 points | c. = 5 points |

5. When someone gives you a compliment for doing a good job, what do you think?

a. Damn right! b. Thank you! You are welcome! c. Amazing! Someone noticed!

| a. = 0 points | b. = 10 points | c. = 5 points |

How Well Do You Know Yourself Scoring Guide

To determine how well "You know You," use the following point value guide to apply the points based upon your responses. Record your score on the "How Well Do You Know Yourself" questionnaire in the column provided on the right side of the page and total that column to obtain your overall score and rating.

SELF ESTEEM. *Give yourself points which correspond with your answer.*

1. Do you have pride in your appearance?

a. = 5 points	b. = 10 points	c. = 0 points

2. Do you believe others deserve dignity and respect at all times?

a. = 0 points	b. = 3 points	c. = 10 points

3. Do you place value on your ethics and reputation?

a. = 0 points	b. = 5 points	c. = 10 points

4. Are you approachable and welcome individuals to come talk to you?

a. = 5 points	b. = 10 points	c. = 0 points

5. Do you dwell on your mistakes and sometimes consider yourself a failure?

a. = 0 points	b. = 5 points	c. = 10 points

Give yourself the corresponding points based upon answering Yes or No.

CONSIDERATION for OTHERS.	YES	NO
Do you treat others with dignity and respect at all times?	5	0
Do you give time or resources ($$) for good causes or charity?	5	0

Do you believe that most people are good at heart and honest?   5   2

When people are rude to you or others, are you rude back to them?   0   5

If you saw someone who was in trouble, would you stop to help?   5   0

DECISION MAKING.

Are you able to access all information for a sound, quick decision?   5   2

Do you consider all outcomes/consequences when making decisions?   5   0

When making a tough decision, can you feel confident about it?   5   3

Do you consider the input of others useful when facing a decision?   5   0

Do you place a high priority on having all the facts before deciding?   5   0

"W.E." Engagement Evaluation

Name:_____Role:_____Date:_____
Time Period: From:_____To:_____Supervisor:_____

To evaluate an individual's level of engagement with W.E. review the following W.E. criteria, circle a score (below), and transfer section Scores to the area below.

Five "W.E." Standards:	Possible Points:	Your Score:
1. Focuses on the job at hand	20	____
2. Doesn't give up or quit.	20	____
3. Shares and bears the work load.	20	____
4. Finishes the job—completely.	20	____
5. Exhibits pride.	20	____
Engagement rating	**Total: 100**	**Total:** ____
- Leadership questions.	20	____
Leadership rating	**Total: 120**	**Leader Total:** ____

- **Focus. Able to focus on their job/work.**

  SCORE
  (lowest to highest pts)

  - o Watches, listens well and learns. 0 1 2 3 4 5
  - o Able to stay on task. Does what is expected. 0 1 2 3 4 5
  - o Identifies what must be done and completes the job. 0 1 2 3 4 5
  - o Follows instructions/directions. Pays attention to their work. 0 1 2 3 4 5

- **Doesn't give up or quit.**

  - o Learns from mistakes. Keeps going even against adversity. 0 1 2 3 4 5
  - o Stays the course. Keeps trying. 0 1 2 3 4 5
  - o Doesn't give up. Not a quitter. 0 1 2 3 4 5

| | | **SCORE** |
| | | (lowest to highest pts) |

o Doesn't let challenges distract them.　　　0　1　2　3　4　5

- **Shares and bears the work load.**

  o A good team player. Doesn't make excuses.　0　1　2　3　4　5

  o Carries and completes their share of the　0　1　2　3　4　5
  work and then some.

  o Are mentally present at their job.　　　　0　1　2　3　4　5

  o Pitches in without hesitation. Makes a　0　1　2　3　4　5
  contribution.

- **Finishes the job.**

  o Does all as expected. Embraces the value of　0　1　2　3　4　5
  follow through.

  o Completes all aspects of their work.　　　0　1　2　3　4　5

  o No half-way work. Finishes up.　　　　　0　1　2　3　4　5

  o Doesn't leave work or trash behind for　0　1　2　3　4　5
  others. Cleans up.

- **Exhibits pride.**

  o Appears self-confident and self-assured.　0　1　2　3　4　5

  o Performs job with superior effort.　　　0　1　2　3　4　5

  o Genuinely proud of successes.　　　　　0　1　2　3　4　5

  o Shares the "good feeling" with others.　0　1　2　3　4　5

Leadership Evaluation: (Complete these questions for Leaders and Diplomats only.)

1. Shows engagement, as a role model, by　0　1　2　3　4　5
exhibiting W.E.behaviors.

2. Provides and receives information well. Keeps an　0　1　2　3　4　5
open door.

3. Treats all individuals with dignity and respect.　0　1　2　3　4　5

4. Appreciates and rewards the efforts of others　0　1　2　3　4　5
regularly and sincerely.

BIOGRAPHY OF LINDA WESTCOTT-BERNSTEIN

Linda is a human resources professional who loves her career choice. She enjoys the opportunity to impact the lifeblood of any company and their employees, in a positive way. She believes effective human resources or human capital management does make a difference and is achieved through meaningful and targeted programs which benefit all employees. Over the years, she has worked in corporate America and prides herself on being a supportive and encouraging boss. She challenges her staff and works with each of them to learn and grow in their careers and to embrace the value of human resources to the bottom line of any company.

She and her husband, Jeff, have lived in Las Vegas, NV for over 20 years and have two grown children. They are life partners and uniquely matched for one another. Both enjoy giving back to their community and hope to instill this desire in their children.

Linda has been involved with the Leukemia Lymphoma Society for Southern Nevada as a Board Member and the American Heart Association in Southern Nevada as Chairman of their Board for three years. She has also been involved with the Smart Grad program, as a volunteer and interviewer as well as volunteered with Special Olympics, Opportunity Village, and United Way of Southern Nevada where she was a Leadership Giver and volunteer.

Linda has three degrees which include an Executive Masters in Hospitality Administration from UNLV, a dual major Bachelors degree in Human Resources Management/Business Administration also from UNLV, and an Associates degree in Liberal Arts from Oakton Community College in Des Plaines, IL.

She worked for over 20 years in the casino gaming industry in human resources management, six years in human resources in the manufacturing industry in Chicago and four years in the travel industry in Chicago.

HUMAN RESOURCES BOOK SERIES

This listing provides the outline for an ongoing series of Human Resources (people-focused) Books by author, Linda Westcott-Bernstein.

It All Comes Down to "W.E."! A Solid Work Ethic is Key to your Success.
-   down to earth lessons in getting your life's work done.

Building your Culture
-   building more than just values and standards to discover who you are.

Business Integrity
-   standing for those things that are good, right, ethical and respectful.

Creativity from the Heart
-   finding your inner beauty and those things that drive you every day.

Customer Service (Notice that "customer" comes first!)
-   putting the customer first; changing the way you treat your clients.

The Value of Community Service
-   giving back in ways that make a difference in others' lives and yours.

Women in Business, A Survival Guide
- helping women navigate the challenges of life in a male dominated world.

Mission:
To provide readers with down-to-earth advice which is based upon life experiences.